REGIONAL DIALECT

REGIONAL DIALECT
AMERICAN SCENE PAINTINGS FROM THE
JOHN AND SUSAN HORSEMAN COLLECTION

JULIE NOVARESE PIEROTTI
WITH AN ESSAY BY KEVIN SHARP

This catalogue is published in conjunction with
Regional Dialect: American Scene Paintings from the
John and Susan Horseman Collection, an exhibition
organized by the Dixon Gallery and Gardens.

Dixon Gallery and Gardens
4339 Park Avenue
Memphis, Tennessee 38117
901.761.5250
www.dixon.org

Photography by Allied Photocolor Imaging Center,
St. Louis

Cover: George G. Adomeit
Tilling the Fields, Zoar, 1941
Oil on canvas over masonite
John and Susan Horseman Collection

ISBN 978-0-9818912-0-0

Printed in Singapore

Exhibition itinerary

Cedarhurst Center for the Arts
Mt. Vernon, Illinois
October 31, 2008 – December 31, 2008

St. Louis Mercantile Library
St. Louis, Missouri
January 24, 2009 – March 8, 2009

The Dixon Gallery and Gardens
Memphis, Tennessee
April 5, 2009 – June 21, 2009

Zanesville Art Center
Zanesville, Ohio
August 1, 2009 – October 13, 2009

Mennello Museum of American Art
Orlando, Florida
November 14, 2009 – February 7, 2010

Morris Museum of Art
Augusta, Georgia
March 6, 2010 – May 30, 2010

Springfield Museum of Art
Springfield, Ohio
June 27, 2010 – September 19, 2010

CONTENTS

PREFACE AND ACKNOWLEDGMENTS

KEVIN SHARP

I first met John Horseman in 2004, when he came to Cedarhurst in Mt. Vernon, Illinois, to see an 1850s Hudson River School painting I had borrowed from a New York art dealer we both knew. When John told me he collected American Scene paintings from the first half of the twentieth century, I wondered why he had made the seventy-mile drive from St. Louis. But after spending an hour with him, I understood completely. No one trolls for paintings like John Horseman. The art dealer who introduced us is no longer with the same gallery, I'm no longer at Cedarhurst, but John is still looking for the next great picture. It's good that there are some things you can always count on.

Without question, John and Susan Horseman have introduced me to as many artists as my art history teachers ever did. John and Susan's astounding knowledge of the great painters who worked in places like Ste. Genevieve, Missouri, Nashville, Indiana, and Zoar, Ohio, during the early twentieth century far outstripped my own, which was not saying much. But after spending ten minutes in John and Susan's home, and seeing painting after painting of unmistakable strength, pathos, and importance, I had to accept that I also knew next to nothing about the lively arts communities that thrived in larger regional metropolises like Cleveland, St. Louis, and Chicago. An interesting new era of my education was about to begin.

Although I had grown up in the very heart of Regionalism country, I some-how had been persuaded that the only American painters worth knowing were either based in New York or boasted a strong exhibition presence there. I had barely finished making excuses for my shallow knowledge of American Scene painting when John explained to me that the painters based in Ste. Genevieve (for example) regularly showed their work in New York – and in other major cities too. I had just missed them. All these years, I simply had been ignoring the names I didn't know in Knoedler, Macbeth, and ACA Gallery catalogues, or in the early Carnegie Internationals, or the Art Institute of Chicago annuals, or the yearly exhibitions in Cincinnati, Columbus, Cleveland, and Washington, D.C. Apparently, once I had found the submissions of Cassatt, Sargent, and Hassam, I had closed the book – and, in so doing, missed the larger story.

These days, the larger story is more accessible and retrievable than ever before. One of the outcomes of our Internet age is that some unjustly forgotten artists from previous periods are attracting a second look, having their achievements reconsidered, and finally receiving their due. With art information Web sites serving as repositories for images and data, with libraries and museums allowing their archives to be accessed online, and with more and more back issues of periodicals and newspapers digitally available, an amazing number of artistic careers have been reclaimed from undeserved obscurity. The populist force of the Internet has empowered us, and it is having a democratizing effect on the way we look at art, artists, and their careers. It may be no coincidence that the painters of the American Scene, some of the most populist figures in the history of art, have been among the first to be uncovered.

John, Susan, and I began to discuss the idea of organizing an exhibition of their remarkable collection in early 2006. Cedarhurst needed a great show to open its new building in the autumn of 2008, and the Horseman collection was a perfect fit. When I accepted the directorship of the Dixon Gallery and Gardens in Memphis in the summer of 2007, I feared that my involvement with the project was over. But once I arrived, I learned that the Dixon had an opening in its exhibition schedule as early as the spring of 2009, which under typical circumstances might have filled me with blind terror. But I knew immediately what I wanted to plug into that vacant slot, and my first call went to John and Susan Horseman.

Not long after I arrived at the Dixon, I hired Julie Novarese Pierotti to be our curatorial assistant and the point person for a show that by then had a title, Regional Dialect: American Scene Paintings from the John and Susan Horseman Collection. Julie is the primary author of this catalogue, and she has skillfully guided the administration of the exhibition. We are very proud of her work on Regional Dialect.

From the outset, John and Susan had expressed an interest in seeing their collection travel to more than one venue. In early 2008, the Dixon put together a proposal for Regional Dialect, along with checklists, images, and timetables, and sent it out to a handful of great museums across the country that had a record of prior interest in American Scene painting. It is a tribute to the quality of the John and Susan Horseman Collection that we were able to secure five venues (in addition to Cedarhurst and the Dixon) for 2009 and 2010, while sending out only thirty prospectuses.

On behalf of John and Susan Horseman and the staff and trustees of the Dixon, I would like to offer our sincerest thanks to the leadership of the excellent venues that are participating in Regional Dialect. We are grateful to Sharon Bradham of Cedarhurst Center for the Arts, Mt. Vernon, Illinois; John Hoover and Julie Dunn-Morton of the St. Louis Mercantile Library; Susan Talbot-Stanaway of the Zanesville Art Center in Ohio; Michael Mennello and Frank Holt of the Mennello Museum of American Art, Orlando, Florida; William S. Morris III and Kevin Grogan of the Morris Museum of Art, Augusta, Georgia; and Angus Randolph and Charlotte Gordon of the Springfield Museum of Art in Ohio.

Whenever you put on a multi-venue exhibition like Regional Dialect and produce a catalogue to accompany it, you invariably find yourself needing assistance and asking any number of favors to bring it to fruition. We have called on many friends and colleagues, and to a person, they have helped us in meaningful ways and on short notice. This, too, no doubt is a reflection on John and Susan Horseman.

Many people in museums and galleries across the country generously provided information on the artists in the exhibition or helped us secure venues for the show. We are most grateful to Angela Solie of Karges Fine Art, Beverly Hills, California; Chris Powers of Bloomington, Indiana; James Reiser of Reiser Fine Art, Carmel, California; Larry Cantor of Lawrence J. Cantor & Co. Fine Art, Century Park, California; Robert M. Hicklin Jr. of Charleston Renaissance Gallery, South Carolina; Patrick Albano and Irene Falconer of Aaron Galleries, Chicago; Michael Worley of R. H. Love Galleries, Chicago; David Lusenhop of Lusenhop Fine Art, Chicago; Jim Keny, Tim Keny, and Darlene Cobb of Keny Galleries, Columbus, Ohio; David Cook of David Cook Fine Art, Denver; Tom French of Thomas French Fine Art, Fairlawn, Ohio; Pat Pierce of Pierce Galleries, Hingham, Massachusetts; Lisa Eckert and Jim Ross of Eckert-Ross Fine Art, Indianapolis; Roberta Haltom and Ray Redfern of Redfern Gallery, Laguna Beach, California; Dave Knoke of Knoke Fine Art, Marietta, Georgia; Derita Williams of Memphis, Tennessee; Gerard and Debbie Davis of Davis Fine Art, Nashville, Indiana; Christine Berry of Spanierman Gallery, New York; Dede Wigmore of D. Wigmore Fine Art, New York; Thom Gianetto of Edenhurst Gallery, Palm Desert, California; Joe Hanon of Ziern Hanon Gallery, St. Louis; David Kodner and Jonathan Kodner of Kodner Gallery, St. Louis; and Bill Williams and Rob Greiner of Lindstrom & McKenney, St. Louis. On behalf of the Horsemans, we offer special thanks to Bill Tregoning of Tregoning Fine Art, Chagrin Falls, Ohio, and Scott Kerr of McCaughen and Burr, St. Louis, who have been instrumental in forming this collection.

We also extend our gratitude to Michael D. Martin of the Flint Institute of Arts, Michigan; Jonathon Stuhlman of the Mint Museum of Art, Charlotte, North Carolina; Sylvia Yount of the Virginia Museum of Fine Arts, Richmond; and Andrew J. Walker of the St. Louis Art Museum. Additionally, we thank Hunt and Donna Bonan, Jonathan Boos, and Jason Schoen for their examples and inspiration.

I would like to extend my personal thanks to the staff of the Dixon Gallery and Gardens for their hard work in bringing this project to successful resolution. My thanks to Harry Baird, Amy Berthouex, Juliana Bjorklund, Melissa Bosdorf, Bill Branch, Barbara Buchanan, Manjula Carter, Maggie Catmur, Marilyn Rhea Cheeseman, Ginny Crittendon, Jenny Duggan, Tanya Dumas, Chris Emanus, Lori Emens, Greg Francis, Sarah Hall, Gail Hopper, Lynn Hulbert, Susan Johnson,

Robert Jones, Kristen Kimberling, Sandra McFall, Norma Montesi, Neil O'Brien, Glenn Overall, Margarita Palmer, Susan Philips, Bobby Rice, Nancy Robertson, Dale Skaggs, James Starks, Janice Tankersley, Nancy Trenthem, and Sharon Williams.

Without the generous support of the Board of Trustees of the Dixon Gallery and Gardens, this project would not have been possible. The Dixon benefits every day from its trustees' leadership and vision, and they make all the work we do here better. To Thomas C. Adams Jr., the chairman of the board during the development of Regional Dialect, to R. Brad Martin, who will be the chairman when it opens at the Dixon, and to all the members of the board, I thank you very much.

I reserve my deepest thanks for John and Susan Horseman. They are visionary collectors who have found a body of work that rings strong and true and in an American key. No painters before the artists of the American Scene and no painters since have been more deeply invested in the American experience or expressed it so clearly and honestly. Because of John and Susan's generosity, thousands of people from all walks of life will experience this moment in American history and this exceptional group of paintings. And whether viewers come from Florida or Ohio or from somewhere in between, we hope they will recognize in the universal language of art their own Regional Dialect.

EDWARD ALDEN JEWELL, JOSEPH VORST, AND THE END OF AMERICAN SCENE PAINTING

KEVIN SHARP

In late October 1941, Edward Alden Jewell, an art critic for the *New York Times*, traveled to Pittsburgh to visit the Carnegie Institute's annual fall exhibition, albeit not the International. "One does miss the Carnegie International," Jewell lamented at the start of his review. "War, waged by one mediocre little landscape artist with a Messianic complex," had finally stopped the flow of modern paintings from Europe and with it, the opportunity for Americans to gain "knowledge of art developments (if any) from abroad." Instead, the Carnegie had put on Directions in American Painting, an exhibition of lesser-known American artists who had never participated in the International. Jewell consoled himself and his readers:

True, this loss is not without its element of gain. During these frightful years we are enabled to give virtually our whole attention to art at home. It is grimly ironic that for a decade or more the eclipse of that attention, for which European leadership was responsible, should have had, in certain quarters, to be deplored. We who believed in American art pleaded that it be given a fair chance to prove itself, and the kind of wholehearted encouragement that might help it grow. We did not ask these boons, however, at such a price.[1]

Jewell was a quintessential insider of the New York art world, a progressive and generous critic and, eventually, an early apologist of the Abstract Expressionists.[2] He was well liked and well respected for his thoughtful opinions, and in his experienced view, contemporary American painting of the 1930s had been overwhelmed by wave after wave of new works by European artists. Artists such as Pablo Picasso,

Henri Matisse, Georges Braque, and Salvador Dalí, no longer *enfants terribles* but the mature (if not venerable) masters of a new modernist age, had effectively driven contemporary American painting from the parlor to the attic.

Jewell had seen it all clearly from his vantage point in midtown Manhattan: the founding of the Museum of Modern Art in 1929, with its ascendance and outspoken preference for European art; the growing number of New York galleries promoting and trading in the European avant-garde; the New York and national media increasingly drawn to sensational and at times outrageous stories about European artists; and the first advance scouts of what would soon become a steady stream of French and German refugee-artists forced by war and persecution to flee their homes.[3] It was not where they preferred to be, but European artists in the 1930s took center stage in the American art world and, in Jewell's opinion, helped drive its schools of regional painting into something akin to irrelevancy.

Jewell had justifiably claimed to be a supporter of American painting, but the arrival and display of so much European art dominated his weekly notices in the *Times*. His less frequent discussions of native painters and sculptors were almost exclusively (and understandably) limited to shows in New York, with occasional summer forays to the art colonies in Gloucester, Cape Cod, and Old Lyme. On the rare occasions when Jewell wished to take the aesthetic temperature of the rest of the nation, he rode the train as far west as Pittsburgh to see the Carnegie International, a show that looked as much like what he could see in Manhattan as anything Middle America had to offer.[4]

Had Jewell traveled more frequently and further into the center of the country in the 1930s, he may have been less surprised by the vigor of the 1941 Pittsburgh exhibition, with its 302 submissions from thirty-one states.[5] He would have found contemporary American art thriving despite the hard times of the Great Depression, and in some cases because of it, as American painters offered meaningful, and by turns sage or humorous, commentary on the trials of a profoundly difficult age. But as Jewell knew better than anyone, the engagement of American artists in their own time and place, in their communities and those who lived in them, was both their greatest achievement and the very reason for their downfall.

American artists had not suddenly become interested in the pleasures and hardships of American existence simply because the stock market crashed in 1929. Trends and developments often do not get named until they are trending vigorously and well developed. That was certainly true of the artistic movement variously described as Regionalism or American Scene painting, or as "the American Wave" by critics who, during the 1931–1932 exhibition season, sought to explain what appeared to be a sudden coalescence of styles and subjects that had infiltrated American painting that year.[6]

It was not as sudden as it seemed. Like most artistic movements, American Scene painting underwent a much longer gestation period than its detractors and even supporters realized. Countless antecedents informed and influenced the way American artists of the 1930s thought about the regions of the country they inhabited and the experiences they portrayed. But perhaps no influence was greater than that of the American landscape painters in the early part of the twentieth century. Having established themselves in such outposts as Brown County, Indiana, and Lindsborg, Kansas, these artists captured the unique and particular identities of their surroundings along with the scenic qualities the areas possessed.

American landscape painting had always been deeply invested in a sense of place. Seeking to do more than awe or inspire with their sublime or picturesque views, American landscapists were engaged in a mission of discovery, like artistic explorers showing a young nation its own great country. Because it was so new (to all but native inhabitants) and because it was so vast and unknown, the North American continent seemed to require more explanation than the terrains of older nations and civilizations. And as nineteenth-century American landscape painting in all its various guises folded into twentieth-century Impressionism, realism, or even abstraction, that explanation seemed to become more precise over time. Coast to coast – and especially in between – artists in regional colonies focused intently on the nature of relatively local landscapes and the existences they supported.

In the first three decades of the twentieth century, many American landscape painters struck a balance in their work between the new European modernism (that was already overturning conventions) and the powerful sense of place the American landscape had always commanded. Artists such as Albert Groll in Arizona, Birger Sandzén in his views of the American West, and Will Vawter in painting after painting of southern Indiana's gently rolling hills introduced increasingly vivid color, robust brushwork, and daring compositional gambits to their canvases. These devices were not so much called into the service of modernism itself but were formal expressions of the regions these artists returned to again and again. The brilliant palette and tactile brushwork of Sandzén's landscapes make them appear quite modern, and they are. But the color and texture of his *Poplars in the Moonlight* (fig. 1), for example, convey something of the startling beauty and rugged power of the New Mexico landscape as well.

When American landscapes of the early twentieth century were transformed into cultivated pastures and scenes of rural labor, their influence on American Scene painting of the 1930s became even more direct. The harvested fields of Adam Lehr and May Ames, the logging subjects of Henry Keller, and the plowing scenes of Elliott Daingerfield and C. S. Price (fig. 2) anticipated as they inspired the painters of the American Scene. The ideal of the pioneer farmer and the virtues of transforming wilderness into crops were enduring elements of American painting since the Hudson River School in the first half of the nineteenth century. That those same motifs would still be viable to artists in the early twentieth century, and that they would experience such an extraordinary flowering in the 1930s, reveals their persistence and durability in the national mythology.

Edward Alden Jewell's belief that influxes of European art in the 1930s had precipitated the declining interest in American painting (and particularly regional American painting) was accurate, but only partly so. The arrival of modern European paintings

Fig. 1
Sven Birger Sandzén
Poplars in the Moonlight, c. 1920
Oil on canvas

Fig. 2
Clayton Sumner Price
Cloudy Evening, c. 1926
Oil on canvas

in volume no doubt created stiffer competition in the marketplace and, more important, in the marketplace of ideas, especially in New York. But on a number of levels, American Scene painters were just as complicit in their own withdrawal from the larger stage.

Through exhibitions and publications, American Scene painting had become by 1932 as firmly established, popular, and critically well regarded as it would ever be. Americans understood that they were settling into a protracted economic depression, and the mostly rural, values-laden, homespun subjects of the American Scene painters seemed to describe the very virtues the country had lost sight of in the urbanization, youth culture, and financial speculation of the roaring 1920s. Even in Middle America, where the Depression, drought, and the Dust Bowl had thoroughly wrecked the agricultural economy and its many ancillary industries, Americans expected their regional paintings to celebrate traditional values and remain unmistakably rural in content.

By the mid-1930s, Americans had already become deeply entrenched in what they expected to see in American Scene painting. And increasingly, Midwestern artists were choosing not to meet those expectations. Playing against type, many American Scene painters of the 1930s eschewed the dusty byways of backwoods hamlets for urban centers like Cleveland, Chicago, and St. Louis. The Ohio artists Carl Gaertner, George Adomeit, Marcelline Spencer, and Robert O. Chadeayne scrutinized their urban and industrial surroundings for the specific qualities that made them unique, just as earlier landscape painters had done and just as the rural painters of the American Scene were still doing.[7] Adomeit's *A Cool, Refreshing Drink* (fig. 3), Spencer's *Cleveland Flats*, and Chadeayne's *Service Station* articulated the American experience as earnestly as the canvases of their colleagues in the countryside. But with factories sitting idle and cities in unmistakable decline, industrial subjects were generally met with tepid responses.

Fig. 3
George Gustav Adomeit
A Cool, Refreshing Drink, 1931
Oil on canvas

Urban American Scene painters were not the only artists to challenge the expectations of their audiences. In 1935, the annual exhibition of American painting and sculpture at the Art Institute of Chicago caused a storm of controversy, with charges of "indecency" leveled not at the nudes in the show but at American Scene paintings. "The suggestiveness which some observers say they discover in facial expressions, contours and attitudes" of the figures in Lester J. Ambrose's *Dime a Dance*, Mary E. Fife's *Lovers on a Stoop*, and Thomas Hart Benton's *Romance*, a painting of a young African American couple holding hands in the moonlight, attracted the sharpest rebukes. But even Doris Lee's prize-winning *Thanksgiving*, depicting a busy country kitchen filled with women preparing the holiday meal, was called "comic" and widely ridiculed.[8]

As the decade advanced and the hard times became harder, American Scene painters, especially those working in the Midwest farm belt, became more overt in their social critique, alienating their regional audiences and even some progressive writers in New York. In 1936, the critic Howard Devree had found "humor and shrewd observation" in the work of Missouri artist Joseph Vorst at the ACA Gallery in Manhattan.[9] A year later, in characterizing one of Vorst's flood scenes at ACA,

Fig. 4
Joseph Paul Vorst
Sharecroppers' Revolt, c. 1940
Oil on panel

Fig. 5
Joseph James Jones
The Pool (Missouri Autumn), 1935
Oil on canvas

Devree noted, "His refugees and fleeing animals are not seen romantically as … those in [John Steuart] Curry's somewhat similar painting, but, rather, presented firmly as a raw event. Such works as these give the show rugged strength."[10] But by 1938, Vorst was beginning to ratchet up his social commentary, sympathetically portraying poor striking sharecroppers (fig. 4), desperate farmers, and devastated families in southern Missouri. Vorst held his first one-person show in New York later that year at the Charles Morgan Gallery, and Thomas Hart Benton wrote the catalogue introduction. By then, Devree had suddenly cooled on the artist and, after noting Benton's introduction, seized the opportunity to unfairly dismiss Vorst's work as derivative, "regretting that these Missouri landscapes and types as presented are so closely allied to Mr. Benton's."[11]

Vorst's friend and fellow Missouri artist Joe Jones received similar treatment at the hands of the New York press. But whereas critics couched their opposition to Vorst's increasingly pointed social commentary by well overstating his debt to Benton, they dismissed Jones's social and political radicalism by complaining that they had seen it much too often. Jones's *Cropper Family* and *We Want More* were described in a 1936 review as "two dark essays which are rather in his earlier vein, perhaps somewhat worked over." The writer blandly continued itemizing, "Social protests against lynchings, evictions, [and] poverty are reflected in several of the canvases,"[12] as if the artist's outcries against such injustices registered as little more than complaining. Jones was only twenty-seven years old in 1936, but already writers apparently had seen enough of his kind of engagement in American life.

Critics, especially those in New York, much preferred Jones when he worked in a more modernist idiom, displaying his ability as a colorist, his understanding of abstract form, and his awareness of all those European paintings arriving in New York Harbor. Certainly, Jewell liked him better that way. In his 1935 review of a group show at the new Walker Gallery on East Fifty-Seventh Street, the writer praised Jones's landscape *The Pool* (fig. 5), "in which he proves that an artist can eliminate all the non-essentials in a scene without eliminating the sense of actuality that is essential to his scheme."[13]

The virtues of essentialism and the reductivist side of modernist aesthetics were already establishing themselves in the consciousness of American art critics. By the time the Guggenheim Foundation was established in 1937 to promote an "abstract type of modern painting," the new American art was moving steadily away from engagement in American life and indeed from any subject matter at all.[14] The latest American vanguard would cast its rebellion in aesthetic rather than social terms: its art would be nonobjective, and its painting would be about nothing so much as painting itself. Jewell approved of the development in his review of the 1940 Whitney Annual:

From beginning to end, the 1940 annual at the Whitney struck me as evidencing a preponderant concern on the artists' part with esthetic and technical problems. This is first and foremost, a *painting* show. And there seemed to me besides to be in evidence a more concerted, more earnestly promoted, trend toward the examination of personal experience; less quixotic rushing afield, into the realm of morning head-line and evening radio bulletin.[15]

Despite Jewell's reservations about those headlines and bulletins as fodder for American painting, they had been consistently dire enough in the 1930s to merit close examination by some of America's most gifted and insightful, if too little celebrated, artists. But the portrayal of class struggle and social injustice during the Great Depression had a shelf life after all, and by 1940, the headlines were about to change again. The early rumblings of war in Europe started the renewal of greater American cohesiveness and whetted an appetite for imagery that was patriotic, or if not patriotic, then not overtly self-critical either – like nonobjective painting.

Even as their audience slipped away, the painters of the American Scene continued their engagement in American life. Joseph Vorst was invited to take part in the 1940 Whitney Annual, where his work was seen once again by Jewell. Although Vorst had been showing in New York regularly the last few years, Jewell had no memory of the artist. So, more out of instinct than observation, he praised and reproached Vorst all in the same breath, and leveled the usual criticism: "I seem not to have encountered before … Joseph P. Vorst … manifestly gifted, though as manifestly, in [the] present work, derivative."[16]

CATALOGUE
JULIE NOVARESE PIEROTTI

LOOKING FOR THE
REGIONAL LANDSCAPE

Arizona Wonderland, 1908
Oil on canvas
40 × 49 inches
Signed lower left: *Groll*
Plate 1

ALBERT LOREY GROLL

American, 1866–1902

Although he trained in Munich and was best known for his panoramic vistas of the American West, Albert L. Groll was born in New York and spent the majority of his career there. Groll's commanding views of the parched New Mexico and Arizona landscape garnered him a good deal of positive attention from the national press and placed him within the inner circle of Manhattan's cultural elite.[1] He was elected an associate of New York's National Academy of Design in 1906 and largely on the strength of his Southwestern subjects, he was made a full academician in 1910.[2]

Groll painted *Arizona Wonderland* in 1908 and may have shown it the following year. He exhibited a number of Arizona subjects in 1909, and they found their way into major shows, including that year's Venice Bienniale.[3] A critic for the *New York Times* might have been commenting on *Arizona Wonderland* when he wrote in his review of the 1909 National Academy exhibition:

Such pictures as … Albert Groll's strongly colored Western subjects … and other canvases of differing degrees of merit but alike in their power to hold themselves aloof from their surroundings, strike sharp, positive notes in a large exhibition, and to a certain extent impose themselves upon the mind, so that it is difficult for the casual observer immediately to readjust his vision for the appreciation of more delicate charms.[4]

Snowstorm, c. 1912
Oil on canvas
25 × 30 inches
Signed lower left: *R. Emmett Owen*
Plate 2

ROBERT EMMETT OWEN

American, 1878–1957

Robert Emmett Owen overcame a disadvantaged childhood in North Adams, Massachusetts, to become a successful artist. Transforming his early talent for drawing into a career in illustration, he published his first drawing in *Life* magazine before his twentieth birthday. Owen settled in New York in 1900 and produced illustrations for most of the city's popular newspapers and magazines.[5] By 1910, he had experienced enough financial reward from illustration to be able to abandon it for landscape painting. He bought a house in the small town of Bagnall, Connecticut, and never stopped finding inspiration in the rural scenery near his home.[6]

Owen probably painted *Snowstorm* two years after his move to Connecticut. Like John Henry Twachtman, the American Impressionist who in the 1890s established himself in nearby Greenwich, Owen was fascinated by the way winter storms transformed the local landscape and light. But whereas Twachtman's winter subjects were delicately composed from subtle shades of white, Owen's canvases captured the experience of the Connecticut winter in all its fierce intensity and blinding, monochromatic force.

The differences between Twachtman's and Owen's concerns were significant and pointed to a new priority taking hold in American painting. Owen was well schooled in the techniques and formal strategies of Impressionist and later Tonalist aesthetics. But in coming of age as an illustrator, he also understood the human impact of a blizzard. No mere formal devices, the sturdy buildings in *Snowstorm* beckon weary travelers to trudge a few more steps to shelter.

A Colorado Sunset, 1916
Oil on canvas
12 × 16 inches
Signed lower right: *Birger Sandzén / 1916*
Plate 3

SVEN BIRGER SANDZÉN

American, born in Sweden, 1871–1954

Birger Sandzén arrived in the tiny plains town of Lindsborg, Kansas, in 1894. By then he had studied in his native Sweden with Anders Zorn, that country's most internationally famous artist, and had spent several months in Paris working with the Post-Impressionist Edmond-François Aman-Jean. In Paris, Sandzén heard his fellow art students from America describe its western expanses, fueling his imagination. He pursued a teaching position at Bethany College in Lindsborg, a community founded by Swedes earlier in the nineteenth century. He would remain in Lindsborg for sixty years.[7]

Sandzén made his first trip to Colorado in 1908, and he would return summer after summer to paint in its foothills and mountains. Although he had found a sense of community and eventually begun a family in the central Kansas town he called home, it was Colorado where Sandzén discovered his greatest inspiration and the subjects for which he would become celebrated. Sandzén may have produced *A Colorado Sunset* directly from life. The composition has all the simplicity and freshness of immediate experience and was built, more than painted, with Sandzén's deft use of a palette knife. The tactile surface quality and his thick application of oil paint in *A Colorado Sunset* were hallmarks of the artist's work, inspired by the rugged western landscape he so admired.

Mountain Splendor, Colorado, c. 1920
Oil on panel
8 × 10 inches
Signed lower left: *Birger Sandzén*
Plate 4

SVEN BIRGER SANDZÉN

American, born in Sweden, 1871–1954

When he moved from Stockholm to the central Kansas town of Lindsborg in 1894, Birger Sandzén brought with him an appreciation of artists working in association for a common purpose, often for the good of the group, but also for the betterment of humanity. Sandzén dedicated his life to promoting the arts. In addition to teaching his students at Bethany College, he organized exhibitions and art clubs both on campus and in Lindsborg, and he regularly donated his works to raise money for scholarships and exhibitions. Late in his career, Sandzén produced murals for the post office in Lindsborg as part of Franklin D. Roosevelt's Works Progress Administration.[8]

Probably painted in the early 1920s, *Mountain Splendor, Colorado* is an intimate sketch of a monumental subject. But Sandzén sacrificed nothing of the scene's power and vigor to the diminutive size of the panel. In the gusto of his robust painting technique and in the density of his impasto, Sandzén imbued *Mountain Splendor, Colorado* with a vitality that expressed the wind whipping the pines and churning the clouds in the Rocky Mountain foothills.

Cedars in the Rockies, c. 1920
Oil on panel
18 × 24 inches
Signed lower left: *Birger Sandzén*
Plate 5

SVEN BIRGER SANDZÉN

American, born in Sweden, 1871–1954

On summer holidays from his teaching duties in Lindsborg, Kansas, Birger Sandzén made nearly annual sketching tours to Colorado's Rocky Mountain wilderness. Probably painted sometime in the 1920s, *Cedars in the Rockies* captures the western landscape that the artist found so striking, while it displays his signature brushwork and aggressive application of oil paint.

A native of Blidsberg, Sweden, Sandzén trained in Stockholm and studied in Paris before moving to Kansas in the mid-1890s to accept a teaching post at Bethany College.[9] His time in the French capital was limited to a few months in 1894, but it was long enough to see examples of the work of Vincent van Gogh, who had died three years earlier. In *Cedars in the Rockies*, Sandzén not only summoned van Gogh's tactile brushwork, expressive color, and luminosity, he also captured something of the spiritual force with which the earlier Dutch artists had painted cypress trees and olive orchards. In Sandzén's work, the azure slopes of the Rocky Mountains and the pale, cloudy sky thrust the twisting forms of two gnarled trees to the foreground of the panel, imbuing these ancient trees with the character of sturdy survivors.

Poplars in the Moonlight, 1919
Oil on canvas
24 × 31½ inches
Signed lower right: *Birger Sandzén*
Plate 6

SVEN BIRGER SANDZÉN

American, born in Sweden, 1871–1954

When Birger Sandzén moved to the United States in 1894, he brought with him the avant-garde painting theories he had absorbed in Paris. With stunning originality, Sandzén adapted these ideas to his new surroundings in the American West.

Poplars in the Moonlight is typical of Sandzén's use of the western landscape to create compositions of extraordinary personal resonance, formal daring, and surprising fidelity to a sense of place. Not unlike van Gogh's cypress trees, the tall, narrow forms of Sandzén's poplars create a repeating rhythm that the artist consciously reinforced with staccato horizontal brushwork. Framed by billowy white clouds that appear to glow more from within than by the light of the moon, these stylized trees appear at the surface of the painting, closing off any view to the low mountains below them. Under a dark blue pointillist sky, Sandzén's poplars are at once an expression of boundary and rigorous abstractions and are wholly suggestive of the western landscapes where they grow.

Cloud Shadows in the Catskills, 1920
Oil on canvas
25 × 34 inches
Signed lower right: *Alex Fournier 1920*
Plate 7

ALEXIS JEAN FOURNIER

American, 1865–1948

A well-traveled landscape painter, Alex Jean Fournier repeatedly sought the support that came with belonging to an association of artists. After studying in France, he became involved in the reformist spirit of the American Arts and Crafts movement, settling in 1903 in East Aurora, New York, at Roycroft, the Arts and Crafts community founded by Elbert Hubbard. When Hubbard died in the sinking of the *Lusitania* in 1915, Fournier left the community and continued his restless travels throughout the United States and Europe.[10]

One of Fournier's favorite destinations was Woodstock, New York, an artists' retreat that had also attracted George Bellows, Robert Henri, Leon Kroll, and other notable American painters in the years after World War I. During his 1920 visit to Woodstock, Fournier painted the mountain scenery and beautiful light effects

of *Cloud Shadows in the Catskills*, perhaps finding the site just a short walk from town.[11] The shadows of unseen clouds passing over a mountain meadow were in their steady movement not unlike the peripatetic Fournier himself. By 1922, he would find himself in Brown County, Indiana, working alongside the community of landscape painters who resided there and generating some of the most original and scenic subjects of his career.[12]

Friendly Neighbors, c. 1921
Oil on canvas
30 × 36 inches
Signed lower right: *Will Vawter*
Plate 8

JOHN WILLIAM VAWTER
American, 1871–1941

Popular among the many artists who settled in Brown County, Indiana, Will Vawter was as well known locally for his good heart and steady drinking as for his art. Vawter had established his reputation as an artist in the 1890s by illustrating the verses of Indiana's most famous – and one of America's favorite – poets, James Whitcomb Riley.[13] Vawter had grown up in Greenwood, Indiana, Riley's hometown, and he had known the celebrated writer since childhood. Vawter's association with Riley and his work would continue for many years, and illustration would remain a vital part of the artist's livelihood well after his paintings had found an audience.[14]

Produced in the early 1920s, *Friendly Neighbors* captures a scene Vawter undoubtedly witnessed many times in rural Indiana. A young woman in a small carriage pulled by a white horse has stopped along a country lane at a small and tidy Brown County farmhouse. Another woman in a white cap and apron stands next to the carriage and appears to chat familiarly with her visitor. Vawter offers no indication of what the two women may be discussing, but it was probably the sort of idle, friendly exchange that took place between neighbors on any given day throughout the year.

Gloucester Harbor, 1929
Oil on canvas
36 × 36 inches
Signed lower right: *B. E. Peters 1929*
Plate 9

BERNARD E. PETERS
American, 1893–1949

For much of the nineteenth century, the Massachusetts port city of Gloucester was a major New England fishing and whaling port and the site of significant shipbuilding. The town boasted busy traffic in its harbor, bustling docks and piers, and steady construction of shingle-style cottages dotting its scenic hills. Since the 1850s, Gloucester had counted among its residents significant American artists lured by picturesque harbor views, affordable lodging, and the town's easy accessibility from Boston. But as the fishing and shipbuilding industries relocated in the 1880s, Gloucester gradually reinvented itself as a resort community, and in doing so attracted some of America's most advanced artists.[15]

By the time St. Louis artist Bernard Peters painted *Gloucester Harbor* in 1929, the city was both an art colony and a crowded tourist destination. Still, Gloucester remained as picturesque as ever. Peters not only captured its beauty and charm, but more than many artists, he was drawn to vestiges of its early identity as a fishing port. Peters painted Gloucester's ships docked for the night where they had once unloaded catches of flounder and cargoes of whale oil. The town's colorful facades and rooftops – once the homes of sea captains, now accommodations for leisure travelers – he pushed into the background.[16]

Untitled (Landscape), c. 1930s
Oil on canvas
36 × 39½ inches
Signed lower right: *B. E. Peters*
Plate 10

BERNARD E. PETERS

American, 1893–1949

An art teacher in St. Louis, Bernard Peters helped found an important art colony downriver in Ste. Genevieve, Missouri, where he painted the Ozarks landscape with exuberant color and brushwork. At an early age, Peters was diagnosed with Bright's disease, an incurable and at that time virtually untreatable kidney ailment, and he did not expect to live through his twenties.[17] Although he was often unwell, sometimes bleak and even difficult, and he frequently isolated himself from his closest colleagues and friends, Peters would live longer than his doctors predicted. On that borrowed time, he produced a large body of landscape paintings that possess not only a deep understanding of the Missouri landscape he admired and so frequently traveled but also a startling expressive strength.

Peters's impressive and seemingly untitled landscape from the 1930s depicts a rustic cabin on the slope of a Missouri hill, which he probably found just a few miles southwest of Ste. Genevieve. Using thick, dark paint thrust into swirling, animated brushstrokes, Peters captured the rugged Ozarks scenery with the vigor of one chopping his way through its thickets and underbrush. Peters worked his paint into tall ridges and deep valleys of impasto that speak to the uneven ground he portrayed. However, the storm clouds massing in the distance also give this commanding canvas a brooding force that may reflect Peters's darker moods.

Untitled (Hills and Rocks), c. 1935
Oil on canvas
29 × 35 inches
Signed lower center: *Ross Braught*
Plate 11

ROSS EUGENE BRAUGHT
American, 1898–1983

Born in Carlisle, Pennsylvania, Ross Braught was a highly regarded young painter who eventually became one of the more eccentric figures in twentieth-century American art. Braught enjoyed early support and recognition when five of his paintings were accepted at the annual exhibition of the Pennsylvania Academy of Fine Arts in 1922.[18] Praised by Thomas Hart Benton and others for his skills as a draftsman and colorist, Braught exhibited widely in the 1920s and accepted a teaching position at the Kansas City Art Institute in 1931.[19] If his work is less well known today than it deserves to be, it is because Braught cut off contact with even his closest friends and colleagues during the last twenty years of his life and at times displayed wildly erratic behavior.

Braught produced *Untitled (Hills and Rocks)* around 1935, the year he rather abruptly resigned from his

position at the Kansas City Art Institute to be immediately replaced by Thomas Hart Benton. The painting's refined surface treatment, its subtle modulation of color, and its elegantly abstracted forms capture the spirit of the western landscape while offering a clear indication of why Braught's work was so admired.[20] In his review of Braught's 1935 exhibition at the Ferargil Gallery in New York, Howard Devree wrote: "Mr. Braught has been challenged by the contours of the eroded lands of the West, and he also reveals a somewhat mystical illustrative slant. It is finished and appealingly decorative work."[21]

The Pool (Missouri Autumn), 1935
Oil on canvas
25 × 30 inches
Signed lower right: *Joseph Jones*
Plate 12

JOSEPH JAMES JONES
American, 1909–1963

Joe Jones's troubled childhood in St. Louis would in no way foreshadow his rise to prominence as an American Scene painter. While still a teenager, Jones ran away to California, winding up broke and under arrest for vagrancy. He eventually returned to St. Louis, taking up house painting with his father, a job that as much as anything led him to an unexpected career as an artist.[22]

Jones's own struggles led him to embrace Marxism, and his paintings, drawings, and eventually murals often exposed the plight of displaced farmers, day laborers, and the working poor left desperate in the wake of the Dust Bowl and the Great Depression.[23] In 1932, he first visited the art colony in Ste. Genevieve, Missouri, an old Mississippi River town south of St. Louis. There, he found artists sympathetic to his political views, and he became the director of the colony's summer art school in 1936. Jones may have painted *The Pool* somewhere around Ste. Genevieve, but it records scenery he could have found almost anywhere in the Missouri Ozarks. From limestone outcroppings, Jones looked down into a slow-moving stream, deep and blue as it twists through the Missouri wheat fields glimpsed in the background. Supporting the trees and lush vegetation on its banks, the stream, in Jones's treatment, is a kind of arcadia, a beautiful respite from a troubled world.[24]

AMERICANS
AT WORK

Corn Shocks (Long Island), c. 1910
Oil on canvas
24 × 36 inches
Signed lower right: *Adam Lehr*
Plate 13

ADAM LEHR

American, 1853–1924

In the fall of 1890, Claude Monet began what would become a large and ongoing series representing the grainstacks he encountered near his home in Giverny. In these canvases, the great Impressionist focused on the effects of sunlight and shadow by examining the play of light on the grainstacks' rounded forms at different times of day and during different seasons of the year. The paintings proved both a critical and financial success, hailed as much for their gentle yet powerful palette as for their rustic representation of the countryside.[1]

The influence of Monet's grainstack series reached well beyond the borders of France. Many American artists found inspiration in the work, including Adam Lehr, a native of Cleveland. Lehr completed *Corn Shocks (Long Island)* around 1910, and by then he may have

seen examples from Monet's series either in the New York branch of Galeries Durand-Ruel or at least in reproduction.[2] Lehr's corn shocks, a distinctly American variation of the grainstack theme, stand tall in a Long Island field amid the pumpkins and their vines that stretch along the ground. More than just a study of light, Monet saw the strength of France in the massing of wheat into great rounded stacks. Similarly, Lehr found something of the American character in the emblematic form of corn shocks stacked for drying.

Logging on the Vermilion River, c. 1910
Oil on linen
39 × 49 inches
Signed lower left: *H. G. Keller*
Plate 14

HENRY GEORGE KELLER

American, 1869–1949

One of America's most influential teachers in the first half of the twentieth century, Henry Keller taught at the Cleveland School of Art for more than forty years and operated a summer academy in the rural community of Berlin Heights, Ohio. Keller had begun his own education in Cleveland in 1887, but he spent much of the 1890s studying in Germany, first in Karlsruhe, then in Düsseldorf, and finally in Munich. He returned to Cleveland permanently in 1902. Keller's experience in Germany and his travels in the rest of Europe lent a cosmopolitan assuredness to his instruction. But he was in no way persuaded by the new modern experiments that were beginning to trickle out of Europe, including Germany, in the early twentieth century, instead emphasizing the basics of color and design.[3]

In *Logging on the Vermilion River*, Keller painted a bleak camp in rural Ohio not far from Berlin Heights. Tall piles of felled trees awaiting transport along the Vermilion River to Lake Erie are stacked to the left side of the composition. To the right, two white draught horses take their ease as a logger trims the next timber to length. Keller's painting of the mud and gray snow of winter captures the flagging spirit of beleaguered men whose livelihood depends on scarring their native soil.

Corn Shocks, Brecksville, 1913
Oil on canvas
23 × 35 inches
Signed lower left: *May Ames / 1913*
Plate 15

MAY LYDIA AMES
American, 1869–1943

Cleveland native May Ames enjoyed a long and successful career as a painter, but she was also an advocate
for the role of women in American visual arts. A member
of the National Association of Women Painters and
Sculptors, she helped found the Women's Art Club in
her hometown. Ames was a well-trained artist, starting
her education at the Cleveland School of Art (she later
returned to teach there) and completing it at the Rhode
Island School of Design. She worked in all genres of
painting, including still life and portraiture, but the subject she returned to most often was landscape.[4]

In *Corn Shocks, Brecksville*, Ames captured a once
common sight in the Midwest landscape. Before the
widespread use of mechanical harvesters, farmers cut
shocks of field corn by hand and then stood them in
tightly bundled cones for drying and easier collection

of the kernels later. Ames painted a harvested Ohio
cornfield just a few miles south of Cleveland, capturing the hazy glow of late afternoon under a soft blue
sky. The warm sunlight of late summer rakes across
and gives dimension to the conical forms as long blue
shadows stretch behind them. Like Claude Monet
painting his grainstacks of the 1890s, Ames reveled in
the dazzling pinks, greens, blues, and yellows created
by sunlight. The extraordinary vigor of her brushwork,
however, was uniquely her own.

The Team, c. 1915
Oil on canvas
24 × 27 inches
Signed lower right: *Elliott Daingerfield*
Plate 16

ELLIOTT DAINGERFIELD

American, 1859–1932

In 1880, Elliott Daingerfield moved to New York from the small town of Fayetteville, North Carolina, to further his career as a painter and writer. There, Daingerfield struck up a friendship with the great landscapist George Inness, who encouraged his protégé to search for a deeper spirituality in his artistic and literary efforts. Daingerfield followed Inness's advice, and for much of his early career he produced images, essays, and poems based on religious themes or with strong allegorical overtones. The most ambitious work he produced in this period was a set of murals for the Church of St. Mary the Virgin in New York City.

Daingerfield eventually grew disgruntled with New York's rapid urbanization.[5] Around 1915, the year he completed *The Team*, Daingerfield moved permanently to Blowing Rock, North Carolina, the mountain town that had served as his summer retreat for thirty years.[6] Increasingly, Daingerfield abandoned the overtly religious subjects that had defined his early career and focused on the beautiful Blue Ridge Mountains that surrounded him. In *The Team*, two mighty draught horses strain as they pull a plow up a steep hillside. The shadowy farmer working the plow lists to the left as he struggles to break newly cleared ground. An important antecedent to the subjects of later American Scene painters, Daingerfield's farmer is cast anonymously but heroically against billowy white clouds that hover over the mountains.

Evening Chores, c. 1920
Oil on canvas
19 × 23 inches
Plate 17

CARL CHRISTOPHER GRAF

American, 1890–1947

A native of Indiana, Carl Graf studied at both the Pennsylvania Academy of Fine Arts and the Art Students League of New York. After completing his education, he returned to his home state with his wife, fellow artist Genevieve Goth, and it was there that his art flourished. He eventually settled among the colony of landscape painters in the picturesque hills of Brown County, Indiana. There, Graf became known for his promotion of the arts in rural Indiana, helping to found the Brown County Art Gallery Association and serving as its first president.[7]

In *Evening Chores*, Graf captured a quiet moment in the barnyard at the end of a working day. In the crisp air of autumn, a woman in a white cap and red shawl greets her farmer-husband while she idly distributes chicken feed to the hens that surround her. Framed in the doorway of an aging rural outbuilding, the farmer prepares to remove the yokes from his two white plow horses after tilling under a field. The farmer's overalls are sagging like the head of one of the horses (and the barn itself), an indication of the hard day they are about to bring to a close. In this ordinary and no doubt infinitely repeated tableau, Graf brilliantly describes the quiet resolve and the steady fortitude of rural people.

Cloudy Evening, c. 1926
Oil on canvas
30 × 32 inches
Signed lower left: *C S Price*
Plate 18

CLAYTON SUMNER PRICE

American, 1874–1950

C. S. Price came of age in the late nineteenth century in a family of Wyoming ranchers, providing him with special insights into the demands, the hardships, and the rewards of rural life. His connection to the soil would remain intact even after he moved to St. Louis in 1905 to pursue his education as an artist. After graduation, Price returned to the West, working first as a magazine illustrator before finally dedicating himself full time to painting.[8]

Price painted *Cloudy Evening* in the mid-1920s, and it captures something of the loneliness and the struggle of farming life. He filled the right side of the composition with a hunched over and exhausted man seated on a riding plow, his two weary horses trudging on before him, as crows circle overhead. The left side of the painting is made up of a large expanse of unplowed field, which the farmer and his team must reach before the night is through. A row of loosely brushed trees lines the field and protects it from western winds, but they also separate the man and his horses from the house and outbuildings that will be their reward for a long night's work.

Barn and Furrows, 1932
Oil on canvas
30 × 35 inches
Estate stamped verso
Plate 19

CARL FREDERICK GAERTNER

American, 1898–1952

Although best known for his views of Cleveland's industrial areas, Carl Gaertner frequently made excursions into the rural Ohio farm country and taught summer classes at the Old White Art Colony in White Sulphur Springs, West Virginia.[9] By 1935, he had become interested enough in rural landscape subjects that he had moved into a house in the Chagrin Valley outside Cleveland.[10] Interestingly, Gaertner's rural subjects often reveal a more modernist and restrained palette and greater formal economy than the urban scenes he painted.

In Gaertner's 1932 *Barn and Furrows*, the artist created a stylized, almost abstract vision of a farm field leading up to a silo and barn. Nearly monochromatic, the neat wide rows receding in perfect perspective are interrupted only by the blank wall of an old, weathered

barn. The pale color of the soil in no way reflects the fertile landscape of Ohio, but provides a subtly toned base from which the imposing form of the silo rises. In *Barn and Furrows*, Gaertner's spare composition and emphasis on repeating pattern is an unusually modern meditation on the cultivated rural landscape, a favorite American Scene subject.

Winter Homestead, 1928
Oil on canvas
31 × 33 inches
Estate stamped verso
Plate 20

CARL FREDERICK GAERTNER

American, 1898–1952

Carl Gaertner was born and reared in Cleveland, he trained at the Cleveland School of Art under Henry Keller – the teacher of so many prominent Ohio painters – and he ultimately became a professor himself at his alma mater. From 1925 until his untimely death in November 1952, Gaertner was a frequent exhibitor at Cleveland's annual contemporary art shows, he participated in Cleveland School exhibitions in New York and Washington, and by the mid-1940s his work was regularly featured in one-person and group shows at the well-regarded Macbeth Gallery, his dealer in Manhattan.[11]

Throughout his career, Gaertner displayed a decided preference for painting winter landscapes blanketed in snow. In *Winter Homestead*, he portrayed a pair of red brick houses connected by a vivid green breezeway in early morning light after a snow. The earliness of the

hour is suggested by the sense of quiet, the absence of any human presence – footprints or otherwise – and the deep snow still clinging to windowsills and chimney tops. Although the sky is dark and gray and may be bringing additional snowfall, the sun brilliantly illuminates patches of snow on the hillside and on the roofs of the buildings, which glow almost unnaturally. In the foreground shadows, Gaertner painted the snow in swirls of luminous blue brushwork, clearly revealing his abilities as a colorist.

Swamp Spur, 1944
Oil on masonite
24 × 40 inches
Signed lower right: *Carl Gaertner 1944*
Plate 21

CARL FREDERICK GAERTNER
American, 1898–1952

During the 1940s, Carl Gaertner frequently rode the train to see his dealer in New York and visit other galleries. He put the time spent in transit to good use by sketching the views from platforms as he waited for trains or out their windows once he had boarded. Painted in 1944, *Swamp Spur* represents a brilliant and poetic final version of one of those sketches. On a cold, gray winter day, a signalman clings to the rail of the caboose, holding steady as the short train comes out of a curve. Flanked by dried cattails rising out of the snow-covered swamp, the lone figure clutches his signal box as the train chugs toward the industrial city in the distance.[12]

In early 1945, Gaertner may have sent *Swamp Spur*, along with similar works, to his first one-person show at the Macbeth Gallery in New York, where a critic noted the exhibition's "decided impact." The review continued: "There are earnestness and integrity in Gaertner's work and he manages to wring reluctant beauty out of an industrial landscape or a seemingly dreary suburban crossing. He has depicted the scene of the terrible St. Clair explosions not as a picturesque piece of reporting but with an underlying sense of human tragedy. 'River Bend' and 'Swamp Road' are none the less individually presented…. This is a decidedly auspicious debut."[13]

Tilling the Fields, Zoar, 1941
Oil on canvas over masonite
25 × 34 inches
Signed lower right: *Geo. G. Adomeit / '41*
Plate 22

GEORGE GUSTAV ADOMEIT

American, born in Germany, 1879–1967

George Adomeit was already a successful commercial artist when he enrolled in the Cleveland School of Art. Completing his education in 1911, Adomeit painted scenes of everyday life around Cleveland and in rural Ohio that were exhibited widely and earned him a national reputation.[14]

In *Tilling the Fields, Zoar*, Adomeit captured the rolling hills of the Ohio landscape near the town of Zoar, Ohio, about seventy-five miles south of the artist's home in Cleveland. Although it was completed toward the end of the Great Depression (and the year the United States entered World War II), *Tilling the Fields, Zoar* does not show fields left barren by farmers evicted from their land. Instead, Adomeit offers an optimistic and almost nostalgic view of rural life as a farmer and his team of plow horses emerge at the crest of one of Zoar's steep hills with admirable determination.

Women Gathering Greens, c. 1937
Oil on canvas
23 × 31 inches
Signed lower left: *McKinnie*
Plate 23

MIRIAM McKINNIE HOFMEIER
American, 1906–1987

Miriam McKinnie was reared in a family of artists who encouraged her ambition to become a painter. In the 1920s, she studied in Kansas City, Colorado Springs, and elsewhere. She was teaching in St. Louis in 1932 when she was invited to exhibit at an art colony in Ste. Genevieve, an old river town sixty miles south of the city along the Mississippi.[15]

Throughout the 1930s, the Ste. Genevieve painters thrived in southern Missouri, and in addition to McKinnie, they counted such notable artists among their ranks as the landscapist Bernard Peters, the German émigré Joseph Vorst, the firebrand Joe Jones, and, for two summers, the great Regionalist Thomas Hart Benton. McKinnie found herself among like-minded painters in Ste. Genevieve, particularly Vorst and Jones, with whom she shared an abiding concern for the struggle of the rural poor. In *Women Gathering Greens*, McKinnie painted three rural wives and mothers collecting the leaves of wild plants for their families' dinners.[16] In June 1937, she sent the painting to New York for the second annual exhibition of Midwestern artists at the ACA Gallery, where the work of Vorst and Jones also appeared. A critic saw the painting and commented upon the "sculptural reality" of McKinnie's heroic figures, who labor anonymously but nobly to sustain their families.[17]

Negro Cotton Pickers, c. 1935
Oil on canvas
35 × 24 inches
Signed lower left: *Hale Woodruff*
Plate 24

HALE ASPACIO WOODRUFF

American, 1900–1980

A pioneering African American painter, Hale Woodruff overcame many cultural obstacles to become one of the country's most prominent artists.[18] Born in Cairo, Illinois, but reared largely in Nashville, Tennessee, Woodruff studied at the Herron School of Art in Indianapolis, where he appreciated the landscapes of the Brown County, Indiana, painters, and at the Art Institute of Chicago. Traveling to Europe in 1927, Woodruff met Henry O. Tanner, an African American artist living in Normandy. Tanner emphasized the importance of the human figure as a form of expression and encouraged his young protégé to return home and battle the difficulties black artists faced in America.[19]

Woodruff reluctantly returned to the United States in 1931 and immediately took a position with Atlanta University. Heeding Tanner's advice, Woodruff instilled in his students the need to break existing racial barriers. He set an important example by exhibiting his work in Atlanta and at major exhibitions throughout the country. Woodruff found inspiration in the history, culture, and struggle of southern African American people, whom he painted sympathetically but never simplistically. Produced around 1935, Woodruff's *Negro Cotton Pickers* presents an image of women working in the fields under a hot, hazy afternoon sky. Sturdy and almost monumental, the woman in the foreground possesses the resolve, the strength, and the dignity that Woodruff found so inspiring.

Silk Stockings and Permanent Wave, 1937
Oil on board
20 × 24 inches
Signed lower right: *Amy Jones 1937*
Plate 25

AMY JONES FRISBIE
American, 1899–1968

Born in Buffalo, New York, Amy Jones studied at the Buffalo School of Art and at Pratt Institute in Brooklyn before launching her career as a painter, printmaker, illustrator, and educator. Despite her achievements in other areas, she may be best known for her murals, which she produced under the aegis of the Works Progress Administration in the late 1930s. President Franklin D. Roosevelt founded the WPA in 1935 both to improve the neglected public buildings and to employ artists, many of whom were struggling to survive during the Great Depression.[20]

Painted about the time that she was producing murals for the WPA, Jones's *Silk Stockings and Permanent Wave* presents an amusing snapshot of American life in the 1930s. A woman, living in an unpainted house with a rusted tin roof and an upstairs apartment, hangs out her laundry on a snowy winter day. Her hair is wound tightly in curlers, and it may be that she is sporting silk stockings under her galoshes, but they lose their allure with such heavy footwear. This trip is not the first the woman has made between clotheslines of frozen laundry as evidenced by the footprints in the snow. In this engaging vignette, Jones insists that even in an economic depression, life's creature comforts – like silk stockings and permanent waves – must occasionally be indulged.

Cotton Pickers Serenade, 1938
Oil on canvas
30 × 42½ inches
Signed lower right: *Alec W. Baird*
Plate 26

ALEXANDER WATSON BAIRD

American, 1910–1990

Little is known about the life and career of the artist Alec Baird. He spent the early years of his career in New York, where he met and married fellow artist Imogen Bowers Groeschel, the daughter of a Scarsdale doctor.[21] Throughout the 1930s and into the 1940s, the Bairds worked in the popular idiom of the American Scene, painting views of everyday life around their homes in Westchester County. Alec was active in the Westchester Arts and Crafts Guild, serving as its president in 1939. The couple circulated with New York artists and struggled to establish careers.[22] In 1949, they finally moved almost five thousand miles west to Honolulu, Hawaii, where Alec found employment as a graphic designer for local produce companies. The Bairds eventually divorced, but Alec remained in Hawaii until his death in June 1990.[23]

Baird completed *Cotton Pickers Serenade* in 1938, when he was still living in Westchester County. The artist seems to have visited but never lived in the American South, and the painting may well have been inspired by the 1936 film version of Jerome Kern's popular musical *Showboat*. Baird portrays African American field workers joined in their labor and song as two of them look back toward the setting sun and prepare to drag their nine-foot sacks in for the evening.[24]

Sharecroppers' Revolt, c. 1940
Oil on panel
24 × 31 inches
Signed lower right: *J. Vorst*
Plate 27

JOSEPH PAUL VORST

American, born in Germany, 1897–1947

The Great Depression of the 1930s may have taken its largest toll on American farmers. The cotton planters and sharecroppers of the South were particularly hard hit as prices plummeted, drought conditions killed yields, and landowners evicted tenant farmers to reduce costs. In 1934, the Southern Tenant Farmers Union was formed in rural Arkansas to promote economic rights for sharecroppers. The union organized a series of protests in 1936 aimed at ensuring fairer wages, more humane working conditions, and decent housing.[25]

In January 1939, sharecroppers in southeastern Missouri walked off their jobs and out of their fields. Evicted or driven from their housing, protesting tenant farmers erected makeshift shacks along the roadsides to make their dissatisfactions known to passersby.[26] Joseph Vorst was working in the southeastern Missouri

town of Ste. Genevieve in 1939 and had great sympathy for the struggle of area tenant farmers. But rather than paint the emotion or the occasional acts of violence the uprising led to, in *Sharecroppers' Revolt* Vorst depicted its very real outcome. No larger-than-life heroes, Vorst's tenant farmers are an ordinary family of five who live in a house made of quilts and huddle around a stove for warmth. The long straight road on the right side of the composition may suggest the protest must go the distance if it is to succeed.

Flood Tragedy, 1940
Oil on canvas stretched on panel
52 × 44 inches
Signed lower right: *J. Vorst*
Plate 28

JOSEPH PAUL VORST

American, born in Germany, 1897–1947

Throughout the 1930s, severe drought threatened the livelihood of thousands of farmers already struggling through the Great Depression. Temperatures soared and strong winds launched columns of dirt hundreds of feet in the air, leading to what became known as the Dust Bowl. In these desperately unhealthy living conditions, almost fifty million acres of farmland were left barren by 1933.[27] Joseph Vorst arrived in Missouri from Germany around 1930. For the next seventeen years, until his untimely death in 1947, Vorst sympathetically portrayed Missouri's rural poor along the Mississippi River, giving visual expression to the struggle for survival on devastated farmland.

As if a cruel antidote to the drought, powerful rainfalls created widespread flooding along the Ohio and Mississippi Rivers in early 1937. Hundreds died and hundreds of thousands were left homeless from Louisville, Kentucky, to Helena, Arkansas.[28] Vorst was amazed by the flood's devastating effects and deeply moved by so many poor people scrambling to save what little they owned. In *Flood Tragedy*, he painted a family in a sturdy wooden boat making for safety through the swirling great river. As they near the shore, the determined man moves to the front of the boat, while his wife nurses their infant child. Two seagulls circling overhead, like Noah's doves, indicate that the waters will soon be receding.

Good Lord Gives Peace, c. 1943
Oil on canvas stretched on panel
48 × 36 inches
Signed lower right: *Vorst*
Plate 29

JOSEPH PAUL VORST

American, born in Germany, 1897–1947

Joseph Vorst was born in Germany and began his career in the troubled 1920s of the Weimar Republic. Like many German artists and intellectuals in the aftermath of the First World War, Vorst was drawn to the populist *völkisch* movement, whose followers hailed rural values as the true German spirit. They celebrated Germany's folk traditions and saw a return to the land as essential to national reinvention. But the *völkisch* movement also spawned a disturbing form of nationalism and noisy rhetoric about Aryan purity that unintentionally fueled the rise of Nazism. Seeing little hope for his country, Vorst moved to America around 1930, settling in an old Missouri town along the Mississippi River called Ste. Genevieve.[29]

Vorst brought the best of *völkisch* sentiment with him to the United States, but he also responded directly and sympathetically to the travails of American rural existence during the Great Depression. Vorst's paintings nearly always focus on rural themes, frequently poverty-stricken African American farmers eking out a living along a mighty but unpredictable river. In *Good Lord Gives Peace*, a ragged and shoeless farmer falls to his knees, praying for strength during a period of blight, signaled by the withering corn stalk behind him. The black cat, a recurring element in Vorst's paintings, may symbolize the misfortune that has been this weary farmer's lot.

THE CITY OF
THE AMERICAN SCENE

Bryant Park, New York City, c. 1910
Oil on canvas
32 × 36 inches
Signed lower left: *Paul Cornoyer*
Plate 30

PAUL CORNOYER
American, 1864–1923

Paul Cornoyer was born and reared and received his early training as an artist in St. Louis. Like many promising painters of his generation, Cornoyer sailed for Paris and in 1889 enrolled at the Académie Julian, where his mature style began to develop. By 1894, he had returned to St. Louis and quickly become one of the city's more popular and sought-after artists. He submitted work to annual exhibitions across the country and was eventually noticed by the great painter and educator William Merritt Chase, who also spent his formative years in St. Louis. Chase purchased one of Cornoyer's paintings and encouraged him to move to New York.[1]

Cornoyer instantly made the streets, parks, and new skyscrapers of New York his preferred motifs. In *Bryant Park, New York City*, Cornoyer painted the popular gathering place behind the New York Public Library in the hazy, suggestive light that would become his trademark. Through an elegant latticework of bare tree limbs, Cornoyer captured the tall *New York Times* building on the right and the Knickerbocker Hotel on the left in the evocative twilight of a winter evening. Figures in the foreground ease into deep shadow, the Sixth Avenue Elevated train trundles past the park, and interior lights flicker on in the restaurants and apartments beyond it, as the setting sun casts an almost heavenly glow on the south face of the *Times* building.[2]

Quatre Arts Ball, 1913
Oil on canvas
36½ × 30½ inches
Signed lower left: *F.G. Carpenter '13*
Plate 31

FREDERICK GREEN CARPENTER

American, 1882–1965

Born in St. Louis, Fred Carpenter studied at Washington University's School of Fine Arts before making his way to Paris to enroll in the Académies Julian and Colarossi, both known for their openness to American students. He remained in the French capital until 1914, but even after returning to St. Louis, Carpenter's style and subject matter would continue to be influenced by his years in Paris.[3]

In Paris, Carpenter immersed himself in French culture and ways of life. He participated fully in the Parisian artistic experience, including the annual Quatre Arts Ball, a scene from which he painted in 1913. Held every spring, the party sent art students, dressed in exotic costumes, parading into the streets of Paris from Montparnasse to Montmartre. The revelry lasted all through the night and ended only with the daylight

hours of the following morning.[4] In Carpenter's painting, three gaily dressed young women in the foreground are preparing their costumes for the night ahead. Brightly colored fabrics of brilliant pattern are strewn on a chaise, a pair of scissors sits at its foot for alterations, and a tall oval mirror waits in the middle distance for finishing touches. The woman in a blue dress shows off a necklace to her friend as a fourth young woman in the background appears ready to join the parade.

Madison Avenue after the Rain, 1915
Oil on canvas
49 × 39 inches
Signed lower right: *Henshaw / 1915*
Plate 32

GLEN COOPER HENSHAW
American, 1880–1946

Glen Cooper Henshaw, born Arthur Glen Hinshaw, grew up in the small town of Windfall, Indiana, and trained at the Herron School of Art in Indianapolis. In the early twentieth century, he traveled to Europe for further study, first in Munich and then at the Académie Julian and the Ecole des Beaux-Arts in Paris. Henshaw remained in Europe until the start of the First World War, when he returned to the United States, settling in New York. Influenced by Whistler and especially by Turner, Henshaw produced poetic vistas of Venice, Lisbon, and Paris before training his vision on the streets of Manhattan, where he kept a studio for much of his career.[5]

Henshaw's *Madison Avenue after the Rain*, completed within a year or two of his return to the United States, is indicative of the artist's atmospheric but distinctive approach to rendering city streets. Painted after a summer rain – the avenue still wet and glistening with reflections – Henshaw's image of the city is one crowded with carriages and hansom cabs racing uptown toward the narrow sliver of blue sky between the skyscrapers. To be so evocative, *Madison Avenue after the Rain* is painted with an extraordinarily bold palette. Between green, pink, yellow, and orange buildings, and under a dazzling blue sky, multicolored carriages squire fashionable urbanites up one of the most famous avenues in America.

Public Square, Cleveland, c. 1919
Oil on canvas
30 × 36 inches
Signed lower right: *W H Kinnicutt*
Plate 33

WILLIAM H. KINNICUTT
American, 1865–1934

Cleveland experienced a great economic and industrial boom in the late nineteenth century, fostering and funding the city's larger cultural ambitions in the first two decades of the twentieth century. The Cleveland Museum of Art opened its doors for the first time in 1916, and the Cleveland Orchestra was founded in 1918. The son of a wealthy Cleveland merchant, William Kinnicutt received formal art training both in his hometown and in New York, where he also studied medicine. He eventually returned to Cleveland, became a member of the Cleveland Society of Artists, and exhibited in the city's annual May Show, if seemingly nowhere else.[6]

Completed around 1919, Kinnicutt's *Public Square, Cleveland* exudes all of the excitement of post–World War I urban America. Crowds of shoppers take advantage of Cleveland's new transportation system to reach

the Public Square, a popular shopping district bounded by Euclid Avenue and crossed by Superior Avenue and Ontario Street. Enticed by the brightly colored billboards advertising everything from butter and cigarettes to a vaudeville house, many of the shoppers were no doubt headed to the May Company, a large department store, which opened on Euclid in 1914. Kinnicutt captured the pleasures of a fashionable mercantile area, but he did not neglect the origins of so much prosperity, as smokestacks rising in the distance belch a gritty haze over much of Cleveland.

Rooftops of Richmond, 1924
Oil on canvas
30 × 34 inches
Signed lower right: *G. H. Baker 1924*
Plate 34

GEORGE HERBERT BAKER

American, 1878–1943

George Herbert Baker spent the majority of his career as an artist painting vivid landscapes in and around Richmond, Indiana. A bustling community of more than 20,000 residents, Richmond supported a rich and diverse cultural life, including an annual exhibition at the Art Association that attracted submissions from across the country. Baker's landscapes were highly praised for their modern spirit; they appeared frequently in Indiana's many venues and at annual exhibitions in Chicago, Cincinnati, Detroit, and New York, earning him frequent prizes.[7]

Baker's bold use of color was often commented upon by critics, and in *Rooftops of Richmond*, the early morning light casts houses and commercial buildings in a pale but radiant orange glow even after the previous night's heavy snow. Baker no doubt viewed Richmond's rooftops from a window of his studio looking out over the old quarter of the city. The gables, flat roofs, and chimneys create syncopated rhythms of geometric pattern, resolving at the tall and distinctive bell tower a few blocks away on North Tenth Street. Snow still clinging to its dome, the tower rises impressively alongside the First Presbyterian Church, its architectural and moral authority unmistakable amid the randomness and makeshift quality of Richmond's rooftops.

Around the Bend, Cuyahoga River, 1925
Oil on canvas
24 × 30 inches
Signed verso
Plate 35

CARL FREDERICK GAERTNER
American, 1898–1952

A native of Cleveland, Carl Gaertner studied under Henry Keller, one of the city's leading painters who taught at the Cleveland School of Art. Like his mentor, Gaertner balanced his work as a painter of quintessentially American subjects with a career as an educator, teaching for almost three decades at the same Cleveland School of Art where he had trained.[8]

Gaertner's hometown and its surrounding areas served as his primary subjects for most of his career. In *Around the Bend, Cuyahoga River*, the artist depicts the industrial area of Cleveland, where the Cuyahoga flows and drains into Lake Erie. On a cold winter day, snow covers much of the densely packed industrial landscape, and tall smokestacks of mills and factories breathe smoke into the crisp Cleveland air. Gaertner's industrial scene is filled with manufacturing, warehousing, and utilitarian buildings, but it is not without its own picturesque quality. As the long shadows of the quiet early morning stretch across pink snow, a large waterfowl paddles in the icy cold bend of the river, casting ripples across the water. In the turquoise river, the red storage tank and the salmon-colored morning light reflecting off the soot and glowing against a brilliant blue sky, Gaertner showed an expressive feeling for color and light as he captured a great American city at work.

Cleveland Flats, c. 1930
Oil on board
27 × 36 inches
Signed lower left: *M. Spencer*
Plate 36

MARCELLINE SPENCER BRUCKER

American, 1910–1986

Marcelline Spencer seemingly sacrificed her own promising career to support that of her better-known husband, Edmund Brucker. Spencer was a native of Cleveland who met and married her husband while he was teaching at the Cleveland School of Art. The couple moved to Indianapolis in 1938, when Brucker accepted a teaching position at the Herron School of Art.[9] Spencer appears to have stopped painting after the move to Indiana, even though the work of her Cleveland years had been impressive and well regarded.

Painted around 1930, when she was still a student, Spencer's *Cleveland Flats* represents the site of the city's industrial boom. The Flats were named for the flat landscape that bounded the Cuyahoga River, and they were home to the steel mills that fueled Cleveland's prosperity. Perhaps ironically, Spencer depicted the Flats as something of a mountainous landscape, with great heaps of slag in the foreground and a huge pile of coal in the middle distance lending her industrial subject the character of a grand manner landscape. However, the crane in the foreground, the coal cars passing endlessly across the composition, and the steel mill washing the hazy Cleveland sky in fiery light more than distinguish the Flats from the Rocky Mountains. Spencer's intentionally and appropriately coarse painting technique aptly conveys the harshness of Cleveland's heavy industry and reveals the unfulfilled promise of her talent.

A Cool, Refreshing Drink, 1931
Oil on canvas
25 × 30 inches
Signed lower right: *Geo. G. Adomeit '31*
Plate 37

GEORGE GUSTAV ADOMEIT

American, born in Germany 1879–1967

During the late nineteenth and early twentieth centuries, the state of Ohio experienced a surge in economic power thanks to the growth of its port cities, its abundant supply of natural resources, and an eager force of immigrant labor and African American workers migrating from the South.[10] As Ohio's urban areas prospered economically, they also became cultural centers that witnessed the founding of art schools, galleries, and museums.

George Adomeit arrived in Cleveland from Germany with his family in 1883, and he benefited from and contributed to the city's effort to balance industry with culture. Adomeit would strike a similar balance in his own career, distinguishing himself as an American Scene painter of first rank while operating his own highly successful commercial art business, the Caxton Company.

In *A Cool, Refreshing Drink*, Adomeit painted the massive piers of Cleveland's High Level Bridge along with a pair of old abandoned houses standing in deep, fresh snow and partially obscuring a vast soft drink billboard in the background. With an adman's eye for the ironic, Adomeit borrowed the title of his painting from the soft drink's slogan while fully realizing that cool refreshment would not be needed on such a cold winter day. Painted in one of the worst years of the Great Depression, the commercial artist in Adomeit may have questioned the effectiveness of a billboard in such a lonely and dilapidated site. But the fine artist in him must have appreciated the poignancy of the scene and the way it captured the mood of the country.

The Old Rock House, c. 1932
Oil on canvas
30 × 24 inches
Signed lower right: *Thalinger*
Plate 38

E. OSCAR THALINGER

American, born in France, 1885–1965

E. Oscar Thalinger was born in Alsace-Lorraine and came with his family to the United States around the turn of the twentieth century. He studied at Washington University's School of Fine Art in St. Louis and then in Munich before returning to America and establishing a studio in St. Louis. He was already a well-known artist in St. Louis in the early 1930s when he discovered and later joined the Ste. Genevieve art colony sixty miles south along the Mississippi River.[11]

Thalinger painted *The Old Rock House*[12] around 1932, at about the same time that he entered the Ste. Genevieve art colony. The Old Rock House was once a significant home on Laclede's Landing in St. Louis, but by the time Thalinger painted it, the abandoned residence was little more than a remnant of a more prosperous era. Like Joe Jones, another artist who divided his

time between St. Louis and Ste. Genevieve, Thalinger frequently made his way to Laclede's Landing to paint the unemployed workers who sought shelter under the bridges as they waited for day labor on the barges. In Thalinger's view of the old quarter of St. Louis, the barges sit idly at the river's edge, two men huddle for warmth on the steps of the house, and a third surveys the snow unmarked by footsteps.

Service Station, 1935
Oil on canvas
30 × 36 inches
Signed lower right: *R. O. Chadeayne '35*
Plate 39

ROBERT OSBOURNE CHADEAYNE

American, 1897–1981

A student and follower of Robert Henri and George Bellows, Robert O. Chadeayne enjoyed a good deal of early encouragement, and his work attracted considerable success in the first part of his career. When he was only twenty-two years old, his *Midsummer Afternoon* was awarded the Norman Wait Harris Medal at the Art Institute of Chicago's annual exhibition in 1920.[13] Chadeayne moved to Columbus, Ohio, in 1927 to accept a teaching post at the Columbus Art School, which eventually led to an appointment at the Ohio State University. For the remainder of his career, Chadeayne worked primarily in and around Columbus.[14]

During his years in Columbus, Chadeayne often painted views of the city's downtown and residential districts, producing vibrantly colored canvases that capture the beauty and simplicity of everyday existence.

In *Service Station*,[15] someone has pulled an automobile – its driver's side door left open – alongside the Standard Oil station. Three men and one woman walk through the unusual intersection and hastily make their way to their respective destinations. The unarticulated features of Chadeayne's figures may speak to the anonymity of modern, urban life in the 1930s, but the scene is bathed in such delightful morning light that it is difficult to imagine a more pleasant community. Chadeayne's work of the mid-1930s, such as *Service Station*, would attract a second round of accolades for the artist.[16]

Ann Arbor, c. 1945
Oil on masonite
26 × 36 inches
Signed lower left: *J. Steele*
Plate 40

JACK KEIJO STEELE

American, 1919–2003

A longtime employee of Ford Motor Company, Jack Steele saw firsthand the effects of heavy industry on the Upper Midwest. Growing up in Detroit, he well understood the importance of the automotive industry to his hometown, his home state, and to the economy of the entire nation.[17] But he also knew the human costs, and his art tended to offer a sympathetic view of the assembly line workers who toiled in Great Lakes factories.

Painted as World War II was coming to a close, Steele's *Ann Arbor* clearly expresses the darkness and even the exhaustion of a Midwestern community after a long and all-inclusive war. Completed as Steele was finishing his own tour of duty as a war artist, *Ann Arbor* depicts soldiers coming home to an unrecognizable country and buildings left abandoned and ruined.[18] Although the American economy experienced a boost in the full employment of the war years, Steele's *Ann Arbor* looks more like a Depression-era community and presents an image of urbanism that was more pessimistic than the hopeful canvases of earlier Regionalist artists. Steele realized that American factories provided much-needed paychecks for thousands of workers eager for jobs in the postwar era. On the other hand, the image of urbanized, industrialized America did not appear to be what the nation had been fighting for during the previous four years.

CHILDREN OF
THE AMERICAN SCENE

Toy Soldiers, 1898
Oil on canvas
25½ × 32 inches
Signed lower left: *T E Butler*
Plate 41

THEODORE EARL BUTLER
American, 1861–1936

The son of a wealthy Columbus, Ohio, businessman, Theodore Butler took advantage of every artistic opportunity that came his way. After studying art in Columbus, he traveled to New York in 1883 to take courses at the Art Students League. In 1887, Butler sailed for France, studying at the Académie Julian and privately with Carolus-Duran, the famous French portraitist and teacher of John Singer Sargent.

Paris provided Butler with an education, but it was the town of Giverny that inspired him. In 1888, Butler and fellow artist Theodore Wendel traveled to the village where Claude Monet had lived since 1883; they received advice and some informal instruction from the Impressionist master, who was less than pleased by the influx of Americans.[1] Butler won his way into the

hearts of the Monet family, and he married the artist's stepdaughter, Suzanne Hochedé, in 1892.

Toy Soldiers, completed a few years after Butler's marriage to Suzanne, depicts their two young children, James and Lili, sprawled on a carpet and lining up wooden soldiers.[2] While Jimmy concentrates on his ranks, Lili looks back at her father, offering a knowing look and concealing one of the French infantrymen from her brother. Butler's paintings of his children in cozy interior settings distinguished him from his famous father-in-law and pointed the way for later American Scene painters engaged in themes of domesticity.

Two Boys Flying a Kite, 1903
Oil on canvas
16 × 11 inches
Signed lower right: *Adam Emory Albright 1903*
Plate 42

ADAM EMORY ALBRIGHT

American, 1862–1957

Adam Emory Albright studied at both the Art Institute of Chicago and the Pennsylvania Academy of Fine Arts in Philadelphia before traveling to Munich and Paris to continue his education. At the Pennsylvania Academy, Albright studied under Thomas Eakins, whose emphasis on human anatomy would influence his student's work for the remainder of Albright's career. Like his great teacher, Albright specialized in figure painting and genre subjects, often depicting his young sons happily playing in dappled Impressionist sunlight.[3]

In *Two Boys Flying a Kite*, Albright portrays two of his sons, complete with straw hats and tattered play clothes, following their kite through the countryside. Working in a loose, painterly style, Albright creates a cheerful image of childhood. His brisk Impressionist brushstrokes reinforce the fleeting nature of childhood, before carefree afternoons are replaced by the responsibility of adulthood.

Play Time (Young Boy), c. 1908
Oil on canvas
38½ × 31 inches
Signed lower right: *A. Schille*
Plate 43

ALICE SCHILLE
American, 1869–1955

Alice Schille studied in her hometown of Columbus, Ohio, and then at the Art Students League and at William Merritt Chase's school in New York from 1897 until 1899. In Chase's academy and later at his summer class in Shinnecock, Long Island, he taught Schille the importance of painting from life, the value of bold brushwork, and the ability to modulate color into subtly shaded variations, all of which she entirely mastered. Ultimately, Chase held his student's work in high enough regard that he acquired two of her paintings for his personal collection.[4]

In Schille's *Play Time (Young Boy)*, the artist painted her dapper subject as if he has just wandered into the room and noticed the artist recording his likeness. A relatively rare interior view – Schille often worked outdoors – this portrait of a toddler in a tan playsuit with red trim, his black stockings pulled up to his knees and his shoes well polished, possesses the freshness and authenticity of an arrested moment. With all the charm of youth, including rosy cheeks and a mop of unruly curls, the young boy looks out with eager, dark eyes and purses his mouth, trying to form some words. Schille's brushwork is by necessity quick and sure, as the little boy seems poised to dash into the next room and out of this charming composition.

The Party Dress, c. 1910
Oil on canvas
39½ × 31 inches
Signed lower right: *A. Schille*
Plate 44

ALICE SCHILLE

American, 1869–1955

Although she never married or had children of her own, Alice Schille proved adept at capturing the essence of young girls and boys – in oil as well as in watercolor, and in portraits and genre scenes alike. Turning up in a variety of poses and compositions, Schille's children always exude an honesty and innocence that is more playful than sentimental and never cloying or trite.[5]

In *The Party Dress*, Schille portrays an apprehensive little girl, dressed in white, who clasps her hands over her heart and looks out with a doubtful demeanor. Backed against a gold-colored wall, she has the flushed cheeks and worried eyes of one who is contrite and about to confess some minor infraction. However, her sweetly penitent expression would suggest that punishment will be light. Schille's subdued palette in *The Party Dress* and her subtle use of white against a largely monochrome background aligns her work with American portraitists a full generation older, such as her teacher, William Merritt Chase, or James McNeill Whistler, or even Cecilia Beaux. But the directness of Schille's portraits and the relative nearness of her vantage point suggest a deeper personal engagement with her subject than commissioned portraiture can typically produce. In this directness of Schille's vision, her portraits point to the connection artists of the American Scene will later find in their own subjects.

Mother and Infant, c. 1910
Oil on canvas
50 × 24 inches
Signed lower right: *Ada W. Shulz*
Plate 45

ADA WALTER SHULZ

American, 1870–1928

Ada Walter Shulz had already chosen to pursue a career as an artist before she married her husband, Adolph Robert Shulz, one of the first painters to visit and work in Brown County, Indiana. Ada met Adolph while studying at the Art Institute of Chicago, and after their marriage in 1894, the couple moved to Wisconsin, where both of their careers began and took flight. The couple traveled frequently to Brown County to paint and to visit friends, and it became their permanent home in the first decade of the twentieth century.[6]

Ada Shulz's many paintings of mothers and children drew upon her personal experience as a wife and mother. But like Mary Cassatt, Elizabeth Nourse, and other artists who explored maternal themes in depth, Shulz's compositions also express the moral and emotional influence women have over their children and the

possibility of creating a better world through child rearing. In *Mother and Infant*, a woman playfully hoists her child into the air, her large and powerful hands securing the baby tightly. The infant smiles and looks back tenderly into the mother's eyes as pale light streams through a window and casts soft shadows on the wall. The very image of contentment and peaceful domesticity, Shulz's painting offers a hopeful theme of a better age ahead.

Mère et Bébé, c. 1912
Oil on canvas
14¼ × 10¾ inches
Signed upper right: *Elizabeth Nourse*
Plate 46

ELIZABETH NOURSE
American, 1859–1938

A native of Ohio, Elizabeth Nourse trained at the McMicken School in Cincinnati before moving to New York in 1882 to further her education at the Art Students League. In 1887, she traveled to Paris and worked at the Académie Julian and privately in the studios of Jean-Jacques Henner and Carolus-Duran. Nourse established her position as a promising young artist through her submissions in the late 1880s and 1890s to major exhibitions in London and Paris. Like Mary Cassatt, she would maintain close ties to the United States while making Paris her primary residence, and she would become one of the few American women painters of the period to earn an international reputation for her work.[7]

Nourse focused her artistic vision on the theme of maternity. Again like Cassatt, she usually chose as her models rural women hardened by years of work along with their plump, healthy babies. Nourse undoubtedly painted *Mère et Bébé* in France, and the work captures the intangible, highly sensory bond between a mother and her child. Painted with long, thick strokes, the woman cradles the ruddy-faced infant in her arms – her nostrils flared as she breathes in the pure and sweet smell of her child. With a rich juxtaposition of well-lit faces against a deep dark background, Nourse captures the essence of this most fundamental of human relationships.[8]

The Reading Lesson (Mother and Daughter),
No. 773, c. 1915
Oil on canvas
28¾ × 23½ inches
Signed lower right: *Pushman*
Plate 47

HOVSEP PUSHMAN

American, born in Armenia, 1877–1966

In Armenia, Hovsep Pushman's parents recognized their son's talent and sent him to the Imperial School of Fine Arts in Constantinople (now Istanbul) at the age of eleven, the youngest student ever at the academy. But when Ottoman Sultan Abdul Hamid II stepped up his persecution of Armenians, the Pushmans immigrated to the United States, settling in Chicago in 1896. Hovsep continued his education in Chicago and later in Paris, where he absorbed the tenets of Impressionism that informed his early style.[9]

When Pushman painted *The Reading Lesson* around 1915, his career was beginning its great ascent. He had won a medal the previous year at the annual Salon in Paris and he would hold his first one-person exhibition at the Art Institute of Chicago the following year.[10] *The Reading Lesson* captures a moment of domestic peace as a woman and child sit in the golden light of a gas lamp and pour over the words on a page. The scene is bathed in the rich color harmony of blues and gold, accented by vases of pink and red flowers on the dresser – harbingers of still-life paintings to come.[11] Pushman once compared painting to storytelling, and *The Reading Lesson* may be a metaphor for the artist's ability to create rich and meaningful narratives.[12]

Bedtime Stories, c. 1915
Oil on canvas
30 × 24 inches
Signed lower left: *Alice Beach Winter*
Plate 48

ALICE BEACH WINTER

American, 1877–1970

Alice Beach Winter and her husband Charles Allan Winter were well-regarded landscapists and portrait painters who also produced illustrations for books and magazines. Their drawings appeared regularly in popular serials such as *Collier's* and *Cosmopolitan* as well as in the graphically innovative journal *The Masses,* a periodical published between 1911 and 1917 that supported the labor movement and socialism and took a strong stance against the First World War. Drawings by both of the Winters appeared frequently in *The Masses,* and Alice eventually became the magazine's art editor. But *The Masses'* opposition to the draft and America's entry into the war led to the federal indictment of its publishers and its all-but-forced closure.[13]

Painted when she was at the height of her involvement in radical politics, Alice Beach Winter's *Bedtime* *Stories* is a charming image of domestic sweetness that reveals the human side of this otherwise firebrand socialist. Winter was well known for her portraits of children, which she often produced in Gloucester, Massachusetts, where the couple spent many of their summers. In *Bedtime Stories*, a woman sits by the glow of a fire, her daughter leaning into her lap. Settling in for the evening, the woman has put down her sewing and managed to remove one of the girl's stockings as she holds her daughter's arm and marks her place in the book with her thumb.[14]

Children on an English Beach, c. 1918
Oil on board
15 × 18 inches
Plate 49

WILLIAM SAMUEL HORTON

American, 1865–died in London, 1936

William S. Horton was born into a prosperous Midwestern family who strongly disapproved of his artistic ambitions. Horton would not be dissuaded, however, and after studying at the Art Institute of Chicago and the Ecole des Beaux-Arts in Paris, he settled in New York to start his career. Horton initially lived the life of a struggling, disinherited artist, but his fortunes changed in 1892 when he married Lorrie Gray. His bride was a New York debutante with income enough to sustain their almost continuous travel to the fashionable European resorts that were Horton's preferred subjects.

When Horton died in 1936, more than one thousand canvases were discovered in his studio, leading some to assume that he never exhibited or sold his work.[15] Horton may have withdrawn from the public stage later in life, but when he painted the delightful *Children on*

an English Beach around 1918, his work was still regularly featured in New York's more prominent commercial galleries. The following year, he sent a group of watercolors and pastels to Knoedler Galleries in New York, where a writer saw them and admired their "very distinguished charm of color and form." The critic was especially drawn to one of Horton's beach scenes: "It would be difficult to find in any work since Whistler's an invention more delicate and free."[16] Like the works of his contemporary, Maurice Prendergast, Horton filled the picture space with mostly female figures dressed brightly in the latest fashions. Also like Prendergast, Horton employed a luxuriously thick impasto technique on his canvas, making the colors and figures pop out of the flat plane of the canvas.

In the Dune Country, c. 1919
Oil on canvas
25 × 30 inches
Signed lower left: *M. B. Titcomb*
Plate 50

MARY BRADISH TITCOMB

American, 1856–1927

The work of Mary Bradish Titcomb attracted collectors as notable and famous as President Woodrow Wilson during the artist's lifetime, but her place in history has undeservedly proven somewhat less secure. In 1886, following the death of her mother, the twenty-eight-year-old Mary Titcomb left behind her life as a schoolteacher in Windham, New Hampshire, and relocated to Boston, where she enrolled in both the Massachusetts Normal Art School and the School of the Museum of Fine Arts. Titcomb may have intended to become an art teacher, but her work sold and her career flourished in Boston.[17]

By 1919, the year she completed *In the Dune Country*, Titcomb had settled into Boston's Fenway Studios, where she counted a number of artist friends, both male and female, among her neighbors.[18] She had come to be identified with a group of local Impressionists, who painted their surroundings in Boston and in nearby Gloucester and Marblehead, the probable setting for *In the Dune Country*.[19] Titcomb employs her typical loose brushwork in this sunny, idyllic composition. Mothers and children amble through the valley of a sand dune, as the chimneys of Marblehead pepper the middle distance and the aquamarine bay spreads in the background. Titcomb's painting conjures a sense of familiar ease and represents its subject with the authenticity of a place experienced often and known intimately.

Untitled (Mother and Child), c. 1935
Oil on panel
27 × 18 inches
Signed lower right: *Vorst*
Plate 51

JOSEPH PAUL VORST

American, born in Germany, 1897–1947

Joseph Vorst is best remembered for his involvement with the Ste. Genevieve Art Colony in southeast Missouri, but he had a lifetime of experience in his native Germany before arriving in the Mississippi River town. He had served in the German army during the First World War and was wounded in battle. During the Weimar Republic of the 1920s, he entered the Academy of Fine Arts in Berlin, but he also witnessed his country's embrace of a dangerous nationalism that would pave the way for Adolph Hitler's Nazi party.[20]

Vorst had known some success in the 1920s, but Germany's increasing intolerance and Hitler's publication of *Mein Kampf* in 1925 and 1926 persuaded him to leave. However, the America Vorst entered was also at a crossroads. With the collapse of the stock market in 1929 and the start of the Great Depression,

Missouri farmers had fallen on hard times and were nearly as vulnerable to extremist propaganda as their counterparts in Germany. In Vorst's mother-and-child composition, a shoeless young mother tends to her infant child as the artist's ubiquitous black cat looks on. Tacked onto the door behind her is a flyer marked "The Savior" with a swastika and an image of Hitler beneath it. Only a German-born artist like Vorst would fully recognize its danger in 1935 and the risks it posed to desperate people.

Smiling Boy, c. 1920s
Oil on canvas
32 × 28 inches
Plate 52

GLEN COOPER HENSHAW

American, 1880–1946

Glen Cooper Henshaw was best known for his atmospheric views of urban settings, but he left behind dozens of portraits that capably capture the likeness and also the spirit and character of the many models who passed through his studio. Bearing the influence of such masters as Rembrandt, Hals, and even James McNeill Whistler, Henshaw's portraits, like those of his contemporaries in the Ashcan school, combine a painterly technique with a willingness to delve into the mind and personality of the sitter. His near-perfect emotional likenesses of men, women, and children from all rungs of society were appreciated by critics and often commented upon in the press. A writer for the *Boston Sunday Post* noted, "Perhaps most outstanding in Mr. Henshaw's work is his ability to capture vividly the most significant quality in a person or scene. In all of his

paintings what seems to interest him most is the meaning behind a face…. Short, swift brush strokes, in the manner of George Luks, aid him in recording the vivid impression."[21]

With its rapid and energetic paint application, Henshaw's *Smiling Boy* creates such a "vivid impression." After calling on Henshaw in his studio, a young boy buttons his coat over a red vest and smiles broadly at the artist as he prepares to leave. It is a perfectly ordinary moment that Henshaw recorded with utter authenticity.

THE GARDEN
AS REGION

Summer Afternoon, c. 1905
Oil on canvas
36 × 24 inches
Signed lower left: *Geo. F. Schultz*
Plate 53

GEORGE F. SCHULTZ

American, 1869–1934

The Chicago artist George Schultz achieved renown for his versatility, and his work appeared at most of the important exhibition venues of his day. His career began as a decorative artist, painting small vignettes on porcelain. Following a summer excursion to Monhegan Island off the coast of Maine in 1895, Schultz began to experiment in watercolor, inspired by the picturesque scenery of the island. He would continue to exhibit his watercolors and oils for the remaining years of his long career.[1]

With its dappled light and shadow, Schultz's *Summer Afternoon* offers countless shades of green in a lush and verdant garden. A thoughtful young woman searches for perfect blossoms on a white lilac bush, which she will clip and arrange in the shallow bowl she holds. The garden is her sanctuary, and she takes refuge in the solitude of its surroundings. Images of beautiful young women dissolving into encompassing gardens proliferated in the early part of the twentieth century. It has been suggested that the ubiquity of the theme may have had some basis in the male desire to equate femininity with nature and an interior life – as opposed to the so-called masculine virtues of intellect and action. But the garden is a complex region all its own, and the lessons of nature and the purposefulness of cultivation are not so easily explained.

Dancing Sunflowers, 1916
Watercolor on paper
19 × 13 inches
Signed lower right: *Chas. Burchfield 1916*
Plate 54

CHARLES EPHRAIM BURCHFIELD

American, 1893–1967

Charles Burchfield completed *Dancing Sunflowers* in 1916, the year he graduated from the Cleveland School of Art, received a scholarship to attend the National Academy of Design in New York, and had his first solo exhibition of watercolors at the Sunwise Turn Bookshop in Manhattan.[2] By then, he was already a visionary, producing watercolors that in their intuitive expression of manmade and natural worlds were unlike the work of any other artist.

Burchfield's *Dancing Sunflowers* combines his own version of realism – a tendency to record ordinary and even intentionally banal subjects – with bold abstraction rooted in an affinity for the spiritual or the fantastic. In this common barnyard setting, Burchfield finds unique patterns that seem equal parts nature and artifice in the play of shadows, in the bowing blossoms, and in the silhouettes of trees and buildings in the upper register of the image. All these elements conform to a sense of the real while subtly inverting it. The stalks, leaves, and blossoms of the sunflowers themselves appear almost skeletal, alternately solid and ghostly.

Burchfield dropped out of the National Academy after one day and moved to Buffalo, where he worked as a wallpaper designer until 1929.[3] Critics eventually responded to his unique vision, he held exhibitions in major museums, and he became the most celebrated watercolorist of the American Scene movement.[4]

The Garden Gate, 1921
Oil on canvas
30 × 25 inches
Signed lower left: *Alice Beach Winter / 1921*
Plate 55

ALICE BEACH WINTER

American, 1877–1970

Like many progressive women at the beginning of the twentieth century, Alice Beach Winter was an active supporter of women's rights, especially suffrage. As the art editor of *The Masses*, a prewar organ of American radical thought, she contributed feminist cartoons aimed at furthering the cause of equality and political representation.[5] Ironically, at the same time that Winter was producing images bound to enflame less liberal-minded women and men, she was also establishing a career as a gifted portrait painter with an affluent clientele.

By 1920, Winter was a well-known and much-in-demand painter of children's portraits. Completed in1921, *The Garden Gate* is a full-length likeness of an adolescent girl in what may be Winter's garden in Gloucester, Massachusetts. Holding a watering can and standing alongside a large and impressive hydrangea bush, the girl in her red plaid dress with white cuffs and collar is in the spring of her own existence, on the verge of blossoming like the giant hydrangea. Winter may have included *The Garden Gate* in a 1922 exhibition of her work at the New York League for the Hard of Hearing on East 59th Street in Manhattan. The twenty-six paintings in the exhibition all featured children, most of whom were set among flowers or in the gardens of Gloucester that provided Winter with so much inspiration.[6]

Dappled Sunlight, 1925
Oil on canvas
32 × 26 inches
Signed lower left: *F. H. Myers*
Plate 56

FRANK HARMON MYERS

American, 1899–1956

Frank Myers was born in the small town of Cleves, Ohio, but his family moved to nearby Cincinnati in 1907 when he was still a young boy. Cincinnati had a long and distinguished history of supporting the visual arts and literature – it was dubbed the Athens of the West in the 1840s – and a surprising number of notable American painters hailed from the Ohio River town.[7] In the relatively prosperous post–Civil War era, Cincinnati's commerce, river trade, and railroad industries flourished, prompting the founding of cultural institutions and further support for the arts.[8]

Myers studied at the Cincinnati Art Academy under Frank Duveneck from 1917 until 1921, when he sailed for Europe to further his education in Paris.[9] He painted *Dappled Sunlight* in 1925, about the same time that he married a Cincinnati schoolteacher named Ella Price,

who perhaps modeled for the composition. In *Dappled Sunlight*, Myers portrays a young woman in a morning dress plucking a small pink flower from her verdant garden. Enveloped by brilliant green foliage and the crowded blossoms of azaleas, hydrangeas, irises, and coneflowers, the young woman contemplates her garden thoughtfully, almost intensely, the hand on her hip suggesting determination more than coquettish allure. No mere ornament of her own garden, this young woman is its creator and caretaker.

Sewing in the Garden, 1925
Oil on canvas
34 × 27 inches
Signed lower right: *Yeteve Smith*
Plate 57

YETEVE SMITH

American, 1888–1957

Highly influenced by George Bellows, her contemporary and a fellow native of Columbus, Ohio, Yeteve Smith overcame many traditional barriers to become a significant modern painter. Working in an era that still found women artists a novelty or, worse, a threat, Smith studied art in Berlin, Washington, D.C., and New York before returning to Ohio to launch her career. She eventually opened a studio in Columbus and came to be admired for her landscapes, still-life paintings, genre subjects, and portraits.[10]

Smith's 1925 *Sewing in the Garden* represents a young woman seated in a beautiful garden, adding stitches to her boldly embroidered jacket. Although thoroughly modern in appearance, the young model is not quite the notorious flapper who scandalized the 1920s. She does, however, wear her hair bobbed in the latest fashion, she sports Mary Jane heels and a brightly patterned blouse, and her red rouged cheeks are a shade deeper than her mother would have chosen. Smith was at least fifteen years older than her attractive model and had come of age before women's suffrage and while other feminist causes were still in doubt. She casts her young visitor in sympathetic light, sewing in a garden, performing a domestic duty that confirmed rather than challenged popular conventions of womanhood. Women's suffrage had brought change, but not the collapse of the social order many anxious Americans expected.

NOTES

EDWARD ALDEN JEWELL, JOSEPH VORST, AND THE END OF AMERICAN SCENE PAINTING

1. Edward Alden Jewell, "Carnegie; Works by Americans, Mostly Unknown," *New York Times*, October 26, 1941, X9.

2. Jewell wrote for the *New York Times*, but he also published essays and novels; in the early 1930s, he authored short biographies on contemporary American artists as part of the new Whitney Museum's publications program.

3. For an excellent analysis of America's embrace of European modern art in the late 1930s, see Martica Sawin, *Surrealism in Exile and the Beginning of the New York School* (Cambridge, Mass.: MIT Press, 1997), 76–102.

4. Jewell covered the Carnegie International every year it occurred, usually with more than one article, between 1929 and 1939. For his first, see Edward Alden Jewell, "New Carnegie International Opens in Pittsburgh," *New York Times*, October 20, 1929, X12. There was no International in 1932.

5. Edward Alden Jewell, "Carnegie Institute Installs U.S. Art," *New York Times*, October 23, 1941, 20. Directions in American Painting was as tilted toward New York as most Internationals. Thirty-one states were represented in the show, but one-third of the submissions came from the state of New York. Unlike at most of its Internationals, the Carnegie Institute acquired nothing for its permanent collection from the Directions in American Painting show. See "Enriching the Collection," *International Encounters: The Carnegie International and Contemporary Art, 1896–1996* (Pittsburgh: Carnegie Museum of Art, 1996), 145.

6. Matthew Baigell, "The Beginning of 'The American Wave' and the Depression," *Art Journal* 27, no. 4 (Summer 1968): 387.

7. Gaertner, Adomeit, and Chadeayne produced more and more rural landscapes in the 1930s. See, for example, the cover of this book.

8. S. J. Duncan-Clark, "Art Exhibit Stirs Storm in Chicago," *New York Times*, November 17, 1935, E7. Doris Lee's *Thanksgiving* was awarded the Mr. and Mrs. Frank G. Logan Prize and $500. It was acquired for the permanent collection of the Art Institute of Chicago. See *Catalogue of the Forty-Sixth Annual Exhibition of American Paintings and Sculpture* (Chicago: Art Institute of Chicago, 1935), no. 123.

9. Howard Devree, "In Local Art Galleries," *New York Times*, May 10, 1936, X8.

10. Howard Devree, "A Reviewer's Notebook," *New York Times*, June 6, 1937, 189. Devree may have been describing *Drifters on the Mississippi*, which Vorst would show again later that year at the Art Institute of Chicago annual, where it was awarded the M.V. Kohnstamm Prize. See *Catalogue of the Forty-Eighth Annual Exhibition of American Painting and Sculpture* (Chicago: Art Institute of Chicago, 1938), no. 234. See also Scott Kerr and R. H. Dick, *An American Art Colony: The Art and Artists of Ste. Genevieve, Missouri, 1930–1940* (St. Louis: McCaughen & Burr, 2004), 98, where the work is titled *Missouri Annual*.

11. Howard Devree, "A Reviewer's Notebook," *New York Times*, November 27, 1938, 178.

12. Devree, "In Local Art Galleries."

13. Edward Alden Jewell, "Younger Artists in Walker Show," *New York Times*, November 30, 1935, 13.

14. "Guggenheim Fund for Art Is Set Up; Promotion of Abstract Type of Modern Painting to Be Its Chief Purpose; Museum Here Proposed," *New York Times*, June 29, 1937, 1.

15. Edward Alden Jewell, "Art in American Life," *New York Times*, December 1, 1940, X9.

16. Ibid.

LOOKING FOR THE REGIONAL LANDSCAPE

1. "Accessions and Notes," *Metropolitan Museum of Art Bulletin* 9, no. 6 (June 1914): 149–153, 150–151. In 1914, the Metropolitan Museum of Art acquired Groll's *Silver Clouds, Arizona*, a painting much in line with and

probably produced around the same time as *Arizona Wonderland*.

2. *History of the National Academy of Design, 1825–1953*, ed. Eliot Clark (New York: Columbia University Press, 1954), 257.

3. Groll's *The Passing Shower: Arizona* was sent to Venice in 1909. See "Art Notes Here and There," *New York Times*, April 11, 1909, X6.

4. "News of the Art World," *New York Times*, March 14, 1909, X6.

5. Lisa N. Peters, *Robert Emmett Owen (1878–1957): The Spirit of New England* (New York: Spanierman Gallery, 1998).

6. Richard H. Love and Michael Preston Worley, *Reflections of Reality: American Paintings from the Hainsworth Collection* (Chicago: Haase-Mumm Publishing Company, 2005), 100.

7. "Dr. Birger Sandzén, Artist of the U.S. West," *New York Times*, June 20, 1954, 86.

8. Marlene Park and Gerald E. Markowitz, *Democratic Vistas: Post Offices and Public Art in the New Deal* (Philadelphia: Temple University Press, 1984), 210–211. Sandzén's work for the Lindsborg, Kansas, post office is entitled *Smoky River* and was completed in 1938. He also painted a mural the next year in Belleville, Kansas, entitled *Kansas Stream*. See also the entry for Amy Jones (cat. 25) for more information.

9. "Dr. Birger Sandzen, Artist of the U.S. West."

10. For more on Elbert Hubbard, see *Head, Heart, and Hand: Elbert Hubbard and the Roycrofters*, ed. Marie Via and Marjorie Searl (Rochester, N.Y.: University of Rochester Press, 1994).

11. Rena Neuman Coen, *In the Mainstream: The Art of Alexis Jean Fournier* (St. Cloud, Minn.: North Star Press, 1985).

12. Ibid., 79. Fournier's early association with Brown County remains somewhat difficult to trace. Fournier and his second wife, Cora Ball, married and settled in South Bend, Indiana, in 1922, after which Fournier visited and painted Brown County more frequently.

13. Lyn Letsinger-Miller, *The Artists of Brown County* (Bloomington: Indiana University Press, 1994), 37–42.

14. Vawter's work as an illustrator was by no means limited to the folksy, homespun values of poets like Riley. In 1915, just a few years before he painted *Friendly Neighbors*, Vawter illustrated George Bronson-Howard's *God's Man*, a dark and provocative story set in New York City. See "New York as Seen by Two Novelists," *New York Times*, September 19, 1915, 20.

15. Richard J. Boyle, "John Twachtman's Gloucester Years," *Twachtman in Gloucester: His Last Years, 1900–1902* (New York: Universe/Ira Spanierman Gallery, 1987), 17–25. Famous American artists who have called Gloucester home include Fitz Hugh Lane, Winslow Homer, Childe Hassam, John Henry Twachtman, and John Sloan.

16. For more on Bernard Peters, see Kerr and Dick, *An American Art Colony*, 221–231.

17. Ibid.

18. Sources claim that Braught, whose physical appearance resembled that of Boris Karloff, often rode around town with a skeleton in his car toward the end of his life. David Cleveland, *Ross Braught, 1898–1983: A Visual Diary* (New York: Hirschl and Adler Galleries, 2000), 10.

19. Ibid., 5–6, 10. Cleveland reports that Thomas Hart Benton called Braught "the greatest living American draftsman," but in the accompanying endnote says that Benton was misquoted and that he actually referred to Braught as the "the greatest living American *craftsman*." Regardless, the most famous American Regionalist held Braught and his work in the highest esteem.

20. Ibid., 10–13. Like Birger Sandzén (cat. 3–6), Braught used his summers away from teaching in Kansas to travel throughout the West, sketching and painting the beautiful and unique landscape there. Braught left behind several sensual landscapes of the Grand Canyon and other western landmarks.

21. Howard Devree, "Briefs from a Reviewer's Notebook," *New York Times*, March 31, 1935, X7. Braught exhibited his lithographs at the Ferargil Gallery in 1935.

22. Kerr and Dick, *An American Art Colony*, 67–83.

23. In addition to painting, Jones, always in support of workers' rights, organized protests and strikes in the Ste. Genevieve area. He also painted murals in post offices in Arkansas, Kansas, and Missouri under the Works Progress Administration.

24. Karal Ann Marling, "Joe Jones: Regionalist, Communist, Capitalist," *Journal of Decorative and Propaganda Arts* 4 (Spring 1987): 46–59.

AMERICANS AT WORK

1. Paul Hayes Tucker, *Monet in the '90s: The Series Paintings* (New Haven, Conn.: Yale University Press, 1989), 65–105. Tucker explores Monet's haystack series in depth in his chapter "Of Hay and Oats and Stacks of Grain: Monet's Paintings of Agrarian France in 1890–91."

2. Claude Monet is believed to have exhibited his works in 1909 at the Sterling-Linder Co. department store in Cleveland. Source: Bill Tregoning.

3. Rotraud Sackerlotzky, *Henry Keller's Summer School in Berlin Heights* (Cleveland: Cleveland Artists Foundation, 1991).

4. Christine Fowler Shearer, Brigitte M. Foley, William H. Robinson, and Judy L. Larson, *Breaking with Tradition: Ohio Women Painters, 1870–1950* (Massillon, Ohio: Massillon Museum, 2005), 24–25, 37.

5. J. Richard Gruber, "Elliott Daingerfield and the Symbolist Spirit, 1893–1916," *Victorian Visionary: The Art of Elliott Daingerfield* (Augusta, Ga.: Morris Museum of Art, 1994), 48.

6. Bruce W. Chambers, *Art and Artists of the South: The Robert P. Coggins Collection* (Columbia: University of South Carolina Press, 1984), 71.

7. Christine Fowler Shearer and Dean A. Porter, *Midwestern Visions of Impressionism: 1890–1930* (Massillon, Ohio: Massillon Museum, 2007), 60.

8. Frank H. Hurley, "C. S. Price: The Development of a Painter (1900–1950)," in *C. S. Price: The Man; The Artist (1874–1950)* (Portland: *Oregon Journal*, 1950), 1–4.

9. "The Summer Schools Announced," *New York Times*, July 1, 1934, X7.

10. Christine Fowler Shearer, "Rediscovering Carl Gaertner," in *Carl Gaertner: A Story of Earth and Steel* (Cleveland: Cleveland Artists Foundation, 2000), 37–47.

11. "Carl F. Gaertner," *New York Times*, November 7, 1952, 23.

12. Shearer, "Rediscovering Carl Gaertner," 44.

13. Howard Devree, "Among the New Art Shows," *New York Times*, January 14, 1945, X8. In mentioning the "St. Clair explosions," Devree was referring to an industrial accident that occurred in Cleveland in October 1944. Gas storage tanks belonging to the East Ohio

Gas Company erupted in a devastating fireball that shot flames 2,800 feet into the air and turned a square mile north of St. Clair Avenue between East 55th and 56th Streets into a ruin. The death toll reached 130. See "Dead in Fire at 83, But May Reach 200; Red Cross Head in Cleveland Gives Estimate as Ruins Continue to Yield Bodies," *New York Times*, October 22, 1944, 41.

14. Shearer and Porter, *Midwestern Visions of Impressionism*, 49; William H. Robinson and David Steinberg, *Transformations in Cleveland Art, 1796–1946: Community and Diversity in Early Modern America* (Cleveland: Cleveland Museum of Art, 1996), 118, 221.

15. Kerr and Dick, *An American Art Colony*, 183–193.

16. Miriam McKinnie's *Women Gathering Greens* was reproduced as *The Gleaners* and dated to around 1940 by Kerr and Dick. The new title and date are based on a review of the painting in an exhibition in New York. See Howard Devree, "A Reviewer's Notebook," *New York Times*, June 6, 1937, 189.

17. Ibid. Earlier in 1937, McKinnie sent *The Cider Press* to the forty-sixth annual exhibition of the National Association of Women Painters and Sculptors, where it was awarded the Celine Baekland Prize for landscape painting. The work was reproduced in the *New York Times*. See "13 Prizes Awarded at Women's Art Show," *New York Times*, January 26, 1937, 23.

18. C. Gerald Parker, "Hale Woodruff Looks Back on Lifetime of Painting," *New York Times*, May 6, 1979, 69.

19. Donald F. Davis, "Hale Woodruff of Atlanta: Molder of Black Artists," *Journal of Negro History* 69, no. 3/4 (Summer–Autumn 1984): 147–154.

20. Park and Markowitz, *Democratic Vistas*. Jones painted several murals for post offices throughout her career, including what is perhaps her most famous mural, *Recording the Victory*, located in the Painted Post, New York, post office. Park and Markowitz list the WPA-sponsored public art in all fifty states as well as Puerto Rico, Washington, D.C., and the U.S. Virgin Islands.

21. Imogen Groeschel Baird was from Scarsdale, and the young couple apparently lived in and around Bronxville and Mount Vernon, New York. See "Westchester Shows Open," *New York Times*, November 25, 1940, 19.

22. See "Arts and Crafts Show Opens," *New York Times*, November 7, 1939, 31. In 1944,

Corporal Alec W. Baird and Imogen Groeschel Baird gave birth to a daughter, Brooke Alexandra. She may have been named in part for her father, but also for Alexander Brook, the New York painter who had also lived in Westchester County (Cross River) and had eventually spent considerable time in Savannah, Georgia. See "Daughter to Alec W. Baird," *New York Times*, July 21, 1944, 22.

23. *Oakland Tribune*, obituary for Imogen Groeschel Baird, April 22, 2007.

24. Derita Williams of Memphis, Tennessee, secured some of the biographical information from conversations with Baird's daughter, Brooke Alexandra Baird Brown. Brown thinks that Alec Baird traveled the South in his youth, but it is also possible that her father visited Alexander Brook in 1938, when Brook was teaching in Savannah.

25. Peter N. Stearns, "Legacy of Resistance: Uncovering the History of Collective Action by Black Agricultural Workers in Central East Arkansas from the 1860s to the 1930s," *Journal of Social History* 32, no. 1 (Autumn 1998): 73–99, 73. See also Howard Kester, *Revolt among the Sharecroppers* (Knoxville: University of Tennessee Press, 1997) for information on the devastating conditions faced by Southern cotton farmers during the Great Depression.

26. John M. Collins, "Distress on Farms Found to Continue," *New York Times*, July 2, 1939, F3.

27. John T. Schlebecker, *Whereby We Thrive: A History of American Farming, 1607–1972* (Ames: Iowa State University Press, 1975), 255–256.

28. "A Relentless Tide: Super-Flood Predicted for the Mississippi 10 Feet above Record; 500,000 Homeless in Ohio," *New York Times*, January 26, 1937, 1 and 2.

29. Kerr and Dick, *An American Art Colony*, 85–97.

THE CITY OF THE AMERICAN SCENE

1. *American Paintings, Drawings, and Sculpture* (New York: Owen Gallery, 2003), 14.

2. Ibid.

3. http://www.rhlovegalleries.com/site/epage/30824_472.htm.

4. "Quatre Arts Ball in Paris," *New York Times*, June 10, 1922, 18.

5. Louise Heritage and Warren Wilmer Brown, *Glen Cooper Henshaw* (Baltimore: Monumental Press, 1945).

6. Love and Worley, *Reflections of Reality*, 68.

7. http://www.waynet.org/ency/artist/bio/baker-george-herbert.htm.

8. Shearer, "Rediscovering Carl Gaertner," 37.

9. Harriet Garcia Warkel, Mark F. Krause, and S. L. Berry, *The Herron Chronicle* (Bloomington: University of Indiana Press, 2003), 101.

10. Robinson and Steinberg, *Transformations in Cleveland Art*, 107. By 1930, the year before Adomeit painted *A Cool, Refreshing Drink*, Cleveland had become the third most populous metropolitan area in the United States, up from a population of 43,000 seventy years before.

11. Kerr and Dick, *An American Art Colony*, 195–207.

12. The painting was reproduced under the title *Ste. Genevieve in Winter* in Kerr and Dick, *An American Art Colony*, 198. My thanks to Scott Kerr for sharing his corrected identification of the building.

13. *Catalogue of the Thirty-Third Annual Exhibition of American Old Paintings and Sculpture* (Chicago: Art Institute of Chicago, 1920), no. 30.

14. Mahonri Sharp Young, foreword, *Paintings by Robert O. Chadeayne: A Retrospective Exhibition Assembled by the Columbus Gallery of Fine Arts* (Columbus, Ohio: Columbus Gallery of Fine Arts, 1973).

15. *Service Station* was included in the 1979 Chadeayne retrospective at the Columbus Gallery of Fine Arts.

16. Chadeayne's work was included in the annual exhibition of the Whitney Museum of American Art in 1937. See "Whitney Museum Annual," *New York Times*, November 5, 1937, 21. His *Oak Street* was included in the 1940 exhibition at the New York World's Fair and the Golden Gate International Exposition in San Francisco. See "Art from All U.S. to Be in Two Fairs," *New York Times*, May 9, 1940, 28.

17. Michael D. Hall and Pat Glascock, *Great Lakes Muse: American Scene Painting in the Upper Midwest, 1910–1960* (Flint, Mich.: Flint Institute of Arts, 2003), 149–150. Steele served as a clay modeler in the styling department at Ford from the late 1940s until his retirement in 1980.

18. Ibid.

CHILDREN OF THE AMERICAN SCENE

1. Katherine M. Bourguignon, "Giverny: A Village for Artists," in *Impressionist Giverny: A Colony of Artists, 1885–1915*, ed. Katherine M. Bourguignon (Giverny, France: Musée d'art American, 2007), 17–28, 23.

2. Charles Stuckey, "American Courtships with Giverny," in *In Monet's Garden: Artists and the Lure of Giverny* (Columbus, Ohio: Columbus Museum of Art, 2007), 47–94, 62. Butler painted several interior scenes of his wife and children in the mid-1890s.

3. Love and Worley, *Reflections of Reality*, 2.

4. William H. Gerdts, *Alice Schille* (New York: Hudson Hills Press, 2001). In addition to being inspired by her early mentor, William Merritt Chase, it appears as if Schille was in conversation with the American post-Impressionist Maurice Prendergast. Schille's watercolors have the same mosaic-like quality that define many of Prendergast's, and the two artists worked at the same time in many of the same areas, including the New England and Normandy coasts.

5. Ibid.

6. Shearer and Porter, *Midwestern Visions of Impressionism*, 65.

7. Mariea Caudill Dennison, "The American Girls' Club in Paris: The Propriety and Imprudence of Art Students, 1890–1914," *Woman's Art Journal* 26, no. 1 (Spring–Summer 2005): 32–37, 35. In appreciation for her service to the American Woman's Art Association of Paris, Mary Cassatt gave Nourse one of her pastel drawings.

8. Mary Alice Heekin Burke, *Elizabeth Nourse, 1859–1938: A Salon Career* (Washington, D.C.: Smithsonian Institution Press, 1983).

9. "Hovsep Pushman Dies at 89; Painter Known for Still Lifes," *New York Times*, February 13, 1966, 84. In 1942, Pushman became only the second artist in the history of the National Academy of Design to turn down an election to its council.

10. See "Notes on Current Art," *New York Times*, April 25, 1920, X10. See also *Special Exhibition of Paintings by Hovsep Pushman* (Chicago: Art Institute of Chicago, 1916).

11. Edward Alden Jewell, "Art in Review: Pushman, a Notable Artist, Shows Some New Canvases and Some Old," *New York Times*, February 10, 1932, 20. Pushman is today best known for the still-life paintings that dominated his late career.

12. "Hovsep Pushman Dies at 89." This obituary quotes Pushman as having said, "When I'm painting, sometimes I feel as wise and as solemn as if I were 100 – then again I am like a dancing, playful child. It depends on the story I have to tell."

13. Rebecca Zurier, *Art for the Masses: A Radical Magazine and Its Graphics, 1911–1917* (Philadelphia: Temple University Press, 1989).

14. "Alice Beach Winter's Exhibition," *New York Times*, April 18, 1922, 33. The papers of Alice Beach Winter are held in the Helen Farr Sloan Library, Delaware Art Museum, Wilmington, Delaware.

15. *The Wonderful World of William S. Horton: American Impressionist (1865–1936)* (Boston: Vose Galleries of Boston, 1966).

16. "Notes on Current Art," *New York Times*, November 23, 1919, XX9. The writer described the work this way: "A group of figures on the Deauville Beach includes one who stands in her bathing suit to have her mantle wrapped about by her maid." It is clearly not the same work in the Horseman Collection, but in the same idiom.

17. Nancy Allyn Jarzombek, "Mary Bradish Titcomb and Her Contemporaries," in *Mary Bradish Titcomb, 1858–1927; Fenway Studios, 1905–1939* (Boston: Vose Galleries of Boston, 1998), 1–21.

18. Ibid., 12.

19. Erica E. Hirshler, *A Studio of Her Own: Women Artists in Boston, 1870–1940* (Boston: MFA Publications, 2001), 144–145.

20. Kerr and Dick, *An American Art Colony*, 85–97.

21. *Boston Sunday Post*, November 29, 1936, quoted in Heritage and Brown, *Glen Cooper Henshaw*, 19.

THE GARDEN AS REGION

1. Love and Worley, *Reflections of Reality*, 114.

2. John Canaday, "Arrived Safely: Burchfield's Journey of Exploration Turns Out to Be a Round Trip," *New York Times*, January 8, 1961, X11.

3. Robinson and Steinberg, *Transformations in Cleveland Art*, 224.

4. Paul Manoguerra, "Charles Burchfield," in *Coming Home: American Paintings, 1930–1950, From the Schoen Collection* (Athens: Georgia Museum of Art, University of Georgia, 2003), 85.

5. Sandra E. Adickes, *To Be Young Was Very Heaven: Women in New York before the First World War* (New York: St. Martin's Press, 1997), 33; Carolyn Kitch, *The Girl on the Magazine Cover: The Origins of Visual Stereotypes in American Mass Media* (Chapel Hill: University of North Carolina Press, 2001), 67.

6. "Alice Beach Winter's Exhibition," *New York Times*, April 18, 1922, 33.

7. Joseph D. Ketner, *The Emergence of the African-American Artist: Robert S. Duncanson, 1821–1872* (Columbia and London: University of Missouri Press, 1993), 34.

8. Edna Maria Clarke, *Ohio Art and Artists* (Richmond, Va.: Garrett and Massie, 1932), 82. The Cincinnati Art Academy was originally founded as the McMicken School of Design.

9. *Frank H. Myers: A Retrospective* (Cincinnati: Art Academy of Cincinnati, 1988).

10. Christine Fowler Shearer, *Breaking with Tradition: Ohio Women Painters, 1870–1950* (Massillon, Ohio: Massillon Museum, 2005).

CHECKLIST

GEORGE GUSTAV ADOMEIT

A Cool, Refreshing Drink, 1931
Oil on canvas
25 × 30 inches
Signed lower right: *Geo. G. Adomeit '31*
Plate 37

Tilling the Fields, Zoar, 1941
Oil on canvas over masonite
25 × 34 inches
Signed lower right: *Geo. G. Adomeit / '41*
Plate 22

ADAM EMORY ALBRIGHT

Two Boys Flying a Kite, 1903
Oil on canvas
16 × 11 inches
Signed lower right: *Adam Emory Albright 1903*
Plate 42

MAY LYDIA AMES

Corn Shocks, Brecksville, 1913
Oil on canvas
23 × 35 inches
Signed lower left: *May Ames / 1913*
Plate 15

ALEXANDER WATSON BAIRD

Cotton Pickers Serenade, 1938
Oil on canvas
30 × 42½ inches
Signed lower right: *Alec W. Baird*
Plate 26

GEORGE HERBERT BAKER

Rooftops of Richmond, 1924
Oil on canvas
30 × 34 inches
Signed lower right: *G. H. Baker 1924*
Plate 34

ROSS EUGENE BRAUGHT

Untitled (Hills and Rocks), c. 1935
Oil on canvas
29 × 35 inches
Signed lower center: *Ross Braught*
Plate 11

MARCELLINE SPENCER BRUCKER

Cleveland Flats, c. 1930
Oil on board
27 × 36 inches
Signed lower left: *M. Spencer*
Plate 36

CHARLES EPHRAIM BURCHFIELD

Dancing Sunflowers, 1916
Watercolor on paper
19 × 13 inches
Signed lower right: *Chas. Burchfield 1916*
Plate 54

THEODORE EARL BUTLER

Toy Soldiers, 1898
Oil on canvas
25½ × 32 inches
Signed lower left: *T E Butler*
Plate 41

FREDERICK GREEN CARPENTER

Quatre Arts Ball, 1913
Oil on canvas
36½ × 30½ inches
Signed lower left: *F. G. Carpenter '13*
Plate 31

ROBERT OSBOURNE CHADEAYNE

Service Station, 1935
Oil on canvas
30 × 36 inches
Signed lower right: *R. O. Chadeayne '35*
Plate 39

PAUL CORNOYER

Bryant Park, New York City, c. 1910
Oil on canvas
32 × 36 inches
Signed lower left: *Paul Cornoyer*
Plate 30

ELLIOTT DAINGERFIELD

The Team, c. 1915
Oil on canvas
24 × 27 inches
Signed lower right: *Elliott Daingerfield*
Plate 16

ALEXIS JEAN FOURNIER

Cloud Shadows in the Catskills, 1920
Oil on canvas
25 × 34 inches
Signed lower right: *Alex Fournier 1920*
Plate 7

AMY JONES FRISBIE

Silk Stockings and Permanent Wave, 1937
Oil on board
20 × 24 inches
Signed lower right: *Amy Jones 1937*
Plate 25

CARL FREDERICK GAERTNER

Around the Bend, Cuyahoga River, 1925
Oil on canvas
24 × 30 inches
Signed verso
Plate 35

Barn and Furrows, 1932
Oil on canvas
30 × 35 inches
Estate stamped verso
Plate 19

Winter Homestead, 1928
Oil on canvas
31 × 33 inches
Estate stamped verso
Plate 20

Swamp Spur, 1944
Oil on masonite
24 × 40 inches
Signed lower right: *Carl Gaertner 1944*
Plate 21

CARL CHRISTOPHER GRAF

Evening Chores, c. 1920
Oil on canvas
19 × 23 inches
Plate 17

ALBERT LOREY GROLL

Arizona Wonderland, 1908
Oil on canvas
40 × 49 inches
Signed lower left: *Groll*
Plate 1

GLEN COOPER HENSHAW

Madison Avenue after the Rain, 1915
Oil on canvas
49 × 39 inches
Signed lower right: *Henshaw / 1915*
Plate 32

Smiling Boy, c. 1920s
Oil on canvas
32 × 28 inches
Plate 52

MIRIAM MCKINNIE HOFMEIER

Women Gathering Greens, c. 1937
Oil on canvas
23 × 31 inches
Signed lower left: *McKinnie*
Plate 23

WILLIAM SAMUEL HORTON

Children on an English Beach, c. 1918
Oil on board
15 × 18 inches
Plate 49

AMY JONES

See under Frisbie

JOSEPH JAMES JONES

The Pool (Missouri Autumn), 1935
Oil on canvas
25 × 30 inches
Signed lower right: *Joseph Jones*
Plate 12

HENRY GEORGE KELLER

Logging on the Vermilion River, c. 1910
Oil on linen
39 × 49 inches
Signed lower left: *H. G. Keller*
Plate 14

WILLIAM H. KINNICUTT

Public Square, Cleveland, c. 1919
Oil on canvas
30 × 36 inches
Signed lower right: *W H Kinnicutt*
Plate 33

ADAM LEHR

Corn Shocks (Long Island), 1910
Oil on canvas
24 × 36 inches
Signed lower right: *Adam Lehr*
Plate 13

MIRIAM MCKINNIE

See under Hofmeier

FRANK HARMON MYERS

Dappled Sunlight, 1925
Oil on canvas
32 × 26 inches
Signed lower left: *F. H. Myers*
Plate 56

ELIZABETH NOURSE

Mère et Bébé, c. 1912
Oil on canvas
14¼ × 10¾ inches
Signed upper right: *Elizabeth Nourse*
Plate 46

ROBERT EMMETT OWEN

Snowstorm, c. 1912
Oil on canvas
25 × 30 inches
Signed lower left: *R. Emmett Owen*
Plate 2

BERNARD E. PETERS

Gloucester Harbor, 1929
Oil on canvas
36 × 36 inches
Signed lower right: *B. E. Peters 1929*
Plate 9

Untitled (Landscape), c. 1930s
Oil on canvas
36 × 39½ inches
Signed lower right: *B. E. Peters*
Plate 10

CLAYTON SUMNER PRICE

Cloudy Evening, c. 1926
Oil on canvas
30 × 32 inches
Signed lower left: *C S Price*
Plate 18

HOVSEP PUSHMAN

*The Reading Lesson (Mother and Daughter),
No. 773*, c. 1915
Oil on canvas
28¾ × 23½ inches

Signed lower right: *Pushman*
Plate 47

SVEN BIRGER SANDZÉN

A Colorado Sunset, 1916
Oil on canvas
12 × 16 inches
Signed lower right: *Birger Sandzén / 1916*
Plate 3

Cedars in the Rockies, c. 1920
Oil on panel
18 × 24 inches
Signed lower left: *Birger Sandzén*
Plate 5

Mountain Splendor, Colorado, c. 1920
Oil on panel
8 × 10 inches
Signed lower left: *Birger Sandzén*
Plate 4

Poplars in the Moonlight, 1919
Oil on canvas
24 × 31½ inches
Signed lower right: *Birger Sandzén*
Plate 6

ALICE SCHILLE

Play Time (Young Boy), c. 1908
Oil on canvas
38½ × 31 inches
Signed lower right: *A. Schille*
Plate 43

The Party Dress, c. 1910
Oil on canvas
39½ × 31 inches
Signed lower right: *A. Schille*
Plate 44

GEORGE F. SCHULTZ

Summer Afternoon, c. 1905
Oil on canvas
36 × 24 inches
Signed lower left: *Geo. F. Schultz*
Plate 53

ADA WALTER SHULZ

Mother and Infant, c. 1910
Oil on canvas
50 × 24 inches
Signed lower right: *Ada W. Shulz*
Plate 45

YETEVE SMITH

Sewing in the Garden, 1925
Oil on canvas
34 × 27 inches
Signed lower right: *Yeteve Smith*
Plate 57

MARCELLINE SPENCER

See under Brucker

JACK KEIJO STEELE

Ann Arbor, c. 1945
Oil on masonite
26 × 36 inches
Signed lower left: *J. Steele*
Plate 40

E. OSCAR THALINGER

The Old Rock House, c. 1932
Oil on canvas
30 × 24 inches
Signed lower right: *Thalinger*
Plate 38

MARY BRADISH TITCOMB

In the Dune Country, c. 1919
Oil on canvas
25 × 30 inches
Signed lower left: *M. B. Titcomb*
Plate 50

JOHN WILLIAM VAWTER

Friendly Neighbors, c. 1921
Oil on canvas
30 × 36 inches
Signed lower right: *Will Vawter*
Plate 8

JOSEPH PAUL VORST

Untitled (Mother and Child), c. 1935
Oil on panel
27 × 18 inches
Signed lower right: *Vorst*
Plate 51

Flood Tragedy, 1940
Oil on canvas stretched on panel
52 × 44 inches
Signed lower right: *J. Vorst*
Plate 28

Sharecroppers' Revolt, c. 1940
Oil on panel
24 × 31 inches
Signed lower right: *J. Vorst*
Plate 27

Good Lord Gives Peace, c. 1943
Oil on canvas stretched on panel
48 × 36 inches
Signed lower right: *Vorst*
Plate 29

ALICE BEACH WINTER

Bedtime Stories, c. 1915
Oil on canvas
30 × 24 inches
Signed lower left: *Alice Beach Winter*
Plate 48

The Garden Gate, 1921
Oil on canvas
30 × 25 inches
Signed lower left: *Alice Beach Winter / 1921*
Plate 55

HALE ASPACIO WOODRUFF

Negro Cotton Pickers, c. 1935
Oil on canvas
35 × 24 inches
Signed lower left: *Hale Woodruff*
Plate 24

Designed and produced by Studio Blue, Chicago
www.studioblue.us

Edited by Leslie Keros

Color separation by Professional Graphics, Inc.,
Rockford, Illinois

Printing and binding by CS Graphics

Typeface is Franklin Gothic